AF264757

Mapping Evolving Internal Roles of the Armed Forces

Albrecht Schnabel and Marc Krupanski

Published by
Ubiquity Press Ltd.
6 Osborn Street, Unit 2N
London E1 6TD

First published 2012

Editors: Alan Bryden & Heiner Hänggi
Production: Yury Korobovsky
Copy editor: Cherry Ekins

DOI: https://doi.org/10.5334/bbr

This book was originally published by the Geneva Centre for the Democratic Control of Armed Forces (DCAF), an international foundation whose mission is to assist the international community in pursuing good governance and reform of the security sector. The title transferred to Ubiquity Press when the series moved to an open access platform. The full text of this book was peer reviewed according to the original publisher's policy at the time. The original ISBN for this title was 978-92-9222-228-4.

SSR Papers is a flagship DCAF publication series intended to contribute innovative thinking on important themes and approaches relating to security sector reform (SSR) in the broader context of security sector governance (SSG). Papers provide original and provocative analysis on topics that are directly linked to the challenges of a governance-driven security sector reform agenda. SSR Papers are intended for researchers, policy-makers and practitioners involved in this field.

The views expressed are those of the author(s) alone and do not in any way reflect the views of the institutions referred to or represented within this paper.

Suggested citation:
Schnabel, A. and Krupanski, M. 2018. *Mapping Evolving Internal Roles of the Armed Forces*. London: Ubiquity Press. DOI: https://doi.org/10.5334/bbr. License: CC-BY 4.0

Contents

Introduction   **5**

Concepts and Methodology   **10**
New challenges, new roles for the armed forces?   10
Methodological challenges of mapping armed forces'
internal roles   14
Towards a heuristic framework   14

Comparative Findings   **17**
Comparative review of evolving "non-traditional" internal roles
and tasks   17
Law-enforcement-related tasks   20
Disaster-assistance-related tasks   29
Environmental-assistance-related tasks   31
Cross-over tasks   32
Miscellaneous community assistance   35
Widely shared reasons behind the armed forces' engagement
in internal roles   38

Comparative Analysis   **41**
Factors determining variation in armed forces' internal roles
and tasks   42
Common traits across the case studies   52
Potential hazards and opportunities of armed forces'
involvement in internal roles and tasks   55

Conclusion   **58**

Notes   **66**

INTRODUCTION [1]

Within a Western paradigm, armed forces have been conceived traditionally as tasked with and restricted to providing external defence, particularly against traditional military threats. This notion of the armed forces as a public security institution dedicated to external defence emerged in the nineteenth century with the rise of the modern nation-state, and became the norm throughout most of the twentieth century. Indeed, during the Cold War armed forces of Western nations were occupied with defence against potential external attacks and focused on external international conflict. However, since the end of the Cold War armed forces of Western nations have increasingly taken on "non-traditional" roles, both internationally in peace support operations and in the form of internal roles and tasks that have typically been assumed to be outside their design, purpose and jurisdiction.

Such a recognizable shift to an engagement in internal roles, particularly within consolidated democracies, presents a notable challenge to a long-held assumption of the roles, legitimacy and purpose of armed forces. Thus far, however, there is a lack of empirical evidence to help parse through and make sense of this development. This paper makes an initial contribution to filling this gap by mapping the internal roles and uses of the armed forces in 15 Western consolidated democracies. Through this exploratory mapping exercise, key factors and common traits are identified that can help in explaining this apparent shift and in understanding the contexts in which internal roles and tasks are performed.

The end of the Cold War more than two decades ago created new international realities, along with hopes and expectations for greater peace and stability worldwide. Part of that peace dividend was expected to be the result of a decrease in defence spending, with direct consequences for the size and functions of nations' armed forces. As a result, in parts of the world that benefited from increased security, the changing security challenges and interpretations of what should be considered suitable tasks and roles of armed forces have led to "profound … shifts in their core roles … [which are] … increasingly challenging long-held assumptions about what armed forces are for and how they should be structured and organized".[2]

Governments and societies have been contemplating the appropriateness of newly defined or previously mainly secondary purposes for their armed forces, which extend beyond their core role of national defence. These include the assignment of a variety of external and internal military and civilian roles and tasks. Some of these are performed as a subsidiary activity in support of operations under civilian command. Mapping, contemplating and analysing these roles inevitably raise questions about their nature, legitimacy and utility, as well as the related interests and motivations of key stakeholders within government, society and the country's security sector. As a result of these processes, countries have developed particular approaches and justifications for such roles.

The focus of this paper is an examination of the internal roles of the armed forces within a selection of Western democracies, the historical background of those evolving internal roles, the legal bases for internal involvement, consideration of other formal security institutions and an attempt to identify preliminary patterns and lessons from those countries' individual historical experiences. This will contribute to a better understanding of why, how and with what results the armed forces play increasingly prominent internal roles in countries that are relatively safe from outside threats.

From this examination, it is evident that armed forces assist in internal security provision mainly as a resource of last resort when efforts are required to respond to exceptional situations. This is the case primarily during and after natural and humanitarian catastrophes as well as other emergencies that exceed the response capacities of civilian and hybrid security institutions. Under the command and control of civilian agencies, the usually subsidiary operations of the armed forces are designed to enhance the capacity of civilian security providers in such situations.

On the other hand, police and gendarmeries[3] in particular, among other security sector institutions such as border guards, intelligence services, private military and security companies and the judiciary, are taking on roles that would in other countries be reserved for the armed forces.[4] A proper understanding of the division of labour between those security institutions, as well as the reasons for evolving shifts in this respect, is helpful in developing approaches that are sensible and draw on the comparative capabilities of a variety of sometimes competing institutions within the same security sector.

It is important to recognize that there are many circumstances in which local, state and federal law enforcement (non-military) routinely handle incidents and scenarios in which the armed forces (military) provide support. This paper is not a normative endorsement of the armed forces' internal roles, but a recognition that in many cases adequate response cannot be provided without drawing on their assistance. In some instances they are called upon to provide additional, subsidiary or at times exclusive action to address a particular scenario. Within standard guidelines, protocols and/or legal frameworks, typically these should be of last resort due to the exceptional nature of utilizing the armed forces, on the one hand, and their perceived or real access to greater resources (i.e. trained personnel, technologies, etc.) on the other.

A number of key terms have been used throughout the paper and its background research, and are defined as follows. First, the term "armed forces" is based on each country's legal basis. In this discussion, "armed forces" excludes hybrid forms such as gendarmeries, unless otherwise mentioned. Second, "security institutions" refer to state security institutions only. Third, "internal roles" of armed forces are those roles and tasks performed within state borders, including maritime boundaries. Fourth, "subsidiary actions" of armed forces refer to roles and tasks performed under the mission leadership of civilian authorities, usually the police.

Moreover, the definitional differentiation between "traditional" and "non-traditional" roles of armed forces is debatable. Roles that are considered as "unusual" or "outside" the armed forces' core business of national defence in one country might be considered traditional practice in other countries. Thus what is thought of as a non-traditional task (and this includes internal roles) in one country might have been a very traditional practice in another. Indeed, armed forces around the world have long served purposes that exceed their "traditional" core role of defending the state from external threats. However, for the purposes of this paper "non-traditional" roles of armed forces are defined as those that go beyond the "traditional core functional imperative of the defence of the state from external threat".[5] According to Timothy Edmunds, "non-traditional" roles include "a number of 'new' or at least newly re-emphasized tasks".[6] He further argues that although "geographically and historically, the centralization of state security provision is the exception rather than the rule" and inter-state conflicts between regular armed forces are almost a remnant of the Cold War era, those are the main security challenges to which "traditional" functions of armed forces are intended to respond.[7] Here the terms "traditional" and "non-traditional" will thus be used with quotation marks, in recognition of the considerable variation that exists across countries in the development and cognition of "traditional" and "non-traditional" roles.

The countries covered in this study are the Western European established democracies of Austria, Belgium, Denmark, Finland, France, Germany, Italy, Luxembourg, the Netherlands, Norway, Spain, Sweden and the United Kingdom, along with the United States and Canada. Choosing countries with similar political systems, understandings and approaches to democratic and civilian governance of the security sector offers a contextual background that allows straightforward comparative analyses. Moreover, for a study that relies primarily on easily accessible information in a limited number of languages, that initial sample proved to be ideal – but not without its limitations, as noted below. Conducting an analysis beyond such a relatively easily manageable set of country case studies would require a different approach, involving collaboration with researchers working in the particular case study contexts and both physical and language access to the sources of information.

This paper is based mainly on research and analysis of academic and policy literature, as well as government documents available electronically in German, English, Spanish or French. In addition, consultative meetings and expert workshops were held with a group of military, police and gendarmerie officers and analysts.

The paper focuses on the analysis of state security providers only, and excludes non-state actors such as private military and security companies or armed non-state actors. In addition, in the research of legal foundations for armed forces' internal roles the paper focuses on internal legal authorities, excluding international and regional frameworks that may have a bearing on the opportunities and limitations of utilizing armed forces in internal roles.

The paper is divided into five sections. Following this introduction, the second section focuses on conceptual considerations as well as distinctions between internal and external security roles provided by armed forces, with reference to the changing roles of domestic security forces such as the police and gendarmerie/hybrid security institutions. It also assesses methodological considerations in greater depth, presenting the heuristic framework that guided this mapping exercise. This framework could serve as a typology for future and more ambitious mapping exercises and analyses. It is designed to analyse both internal and external (referred to in that framework as "internal" and "international") "non-traditional" roles and tasks of the armed forces. In addition to this broader typology, a narrower version is presented, which was used to analyse the case studies covered in this mapping exercise. The third section focuses on the empirical evidence obtained from the 15 case studies. The most common internal roles are introduced, along with examples from the case studies covered in the mapping exercise. Furthermore, key driving forces behind the armed forces' engagement in internal tasks are highlighted. The fourth section reports on the analysis of the mapping exercise, including a number of central factors that help explain variation among armed forces' internal roles and tasks as well as common traits across the case studies. It also examines potential hazards and opportunities for utilizing armed forces for internal roles and tasks. The final section discusses the mapping exercise's significance for practitioners and researchers, and provides a review of the key findings of this paper.

CONCEPTS AND METHOLODOGY

This section outlines evolving new challenges and roles of the armed forces, with a focus on tasks performed inside their country's borders. This is followed by a proposal to map those internal roles, which involves a number of challenges. The section concludes with the presentation of a heuristic framework developed to map "non-traditional" roles and tasks of armed forces. While the framework can be used to map both external and internal roles, the subsequent empirical section of this paper focuses on internal roles only.

New challenges, new roles for the armed forces?

It has become a common assumption that the role of the armed forces, especially among consolidated Western democracies, is to provide security against external threats, while police forces are tasked with providing internal security, surveillance and order inside a country's borders. The distinction between external and internal security, as well as between the respective responsibilities of individual public security institutions, has been well documented,[8] even to the point of what Keith Krause calls a "seemingly natural division".[9] Of course, this division was not the product of a coherent process, nor did it innately appear. As Charles Tilly suggests, armies frequently served the purpose of consolidating wealth and power of princes, often at the expense of and in direct confrontation with the domestic population.[10] In fact, it is commonly understood that the demarcation between external and internal roles of public security institutions (in particular armed forces and police, respectively) was not generally accepted and normalized until "the spread of modern nationalism in the 19th century … [when] the boundaries between external and domestic start to coincide with formal legal frontiers".[11] Such an understanding of the clear boundaries between internal and external security provision and providers remained through most of the twentieth century, especially during the Cold War period. During this time, while most nations braced themselves for anticipated imminent international conflict, this division seemed apparent and almost natural.

The end of the Cold War, however, triggered new security threats which challenged the "traditional" roles assumed by armed forces, especially within consolidated Western democracies. During the early stages of the Cold War the main priority of security provision in the Euro-Atlantic area was the search for the most appropriate response to a broad spectrum of military, ideological, political, social and economic challenges from the Soviet Union. Under the pressure of the ensuing nuclear arms race this initially wide conceptualization was narrowed down to a largely military focus – and thus national and regional security provision became the prime task of states' armed forces and the military strategies of individual states and their security alliances. To be sure, during the Cold War a substantial and identifiable military threat existed, providing the rationale for considerable defence spending. The arms race between East and West was not only about the quality and quantity of arms, but also about which side (i.e. political, ideological and economic system) could withstand the greater financial sacrifices needed to remain politically and militarily competitive. Moreover, during this period the focus was primarily on deterring and managing inter-state conflicts, which encouraged the maintenance of adequately armed military forces for both deterrence and combat operations, if needed. These threats were also the main focus of regional military alliances and, for that matter, United Nations involvement in traditional peacekeeping as well as Chapter VII military operations. Other parallel realities of course existed, such as internal conflicts (genuine intra-state wars and proxy wars of the superpowers) and various internal roles of armed forces that were unrelated to the suppression of internal violence or the deterrence of external threats. However, those non-traditional activities were overshadowed by Cold War priorities.[12]

After the likelihood of war between East and West faded away with the dissolution of the Soviet Union in 1991, predominant realist assumptions about the primacy of military security became less pronounced in national and international policy debates. The concept of security utilized by most Western states expanded to include a broader variety of threats (such as environmental or economic threats) at increasingly diverse levels of analysis above and below the state. Official security discourses during the Cold War, focused primarily on national security, gave way to a more nuanced understanding of security needs beyond the individual state (at the regional and international levels) as well as below the state (at the levels of communities and individuals).[13] "Deterrence" has since been taking on a different, more subtle meaning: human rights provision assures human security; development assistance supports economic security; long-term investments in environmental protection facilitate sustainable environmental security; and the alleviation of poverty serves as a strategy to prevent violent community-based conflict. Moreover, international cooperation is increasingly considered to be the most effective approach to the prevention of inter-state and intra-state conflict and a plethora of new security challenges, including the growing fear of global terrorism.

The end of the Cold War was accompanied by widespread societal and political expectations for a considerable peace dividend, which carried consequences for states' armed forces, including calls for their downsizing and decreased military and defence spending. As Timothy Edmunds argues, at first "the end of the Cold War removed the dominant strategic lens through which armed forces were developed and understood, and has entailed a fundamental reconsideration of their purpose and the bases for legitimacy across the [European] continent".[14] This has triggered wide-ranging defence reviews, significant cuts in military budgets and societal scrutiny of the armed forces' roles, tasks and purposes.[15] Second, particularly in the wake of the dissolution of the former Yugoslavia, the "traditional" roles of armed forces have been challenged in the context of ethnic and civil conflict, in terms of both the roles of national armed forces as conflict parties and the involvement of external armed forces in international peace operations. Third, the terrorist attacks of 11 September 2001 "reinforced existing pressures towards the development of expeditionary capabilities in reforming armed forces … [which are] …

illustrative of the emerging dominance of Anglo-American concepts of military professionalization in the wider security sector reform area", along with counter-insurgency and internal security tasks of the armed forces.[16] The focus on the war on terror has also challenged the armed forces' previous status as the primary organization capable of defending a state against external – terrorist – attacks. According to Edmunds, intelligence, border and police forces "may be more suited to meeting day-to-day operational challenges posed by international terrorism, and over the long-term the utility of the military in this role may be limited".[17]

This final point on the heightened perceived threat of terrorism deserves further discussion. Although expectations for a peace dividend due to the end of the Cold War put pressure on states to downsize their armed forces, new and diverse military commitments proliferated considerably. National defence strategies now placed emphasis on the so-called "war on terror" and the deterrence of terrorist threats, which put an increased importance on the role of armed forces and – contrary to expectations – increased defence spending (particularly in the US). These newly defined national security priorities included the need to be prepared to prevent, deter, coerce, disrupt or destroy international terrorists or the regimes that harboured them and to counter terrorists' efforts to acquire chemical, biological, radiological and nuclear weapons. Multilateral peace and stabilization operations and defence diplomacy were seen as important assets in addressing the causes and symptoms of conflict and terrorism.[18] Numerous crises – ranging from Kosovo to Macedonia, Sierra Leone, East Timor, Afghanistan, the Democratic Republic of the Congo, Iraq and, most recently, Libya – have demonstrated that the global security environment was to be as uncertain as ever and armed forces were facing an even broader range, frequency and often duration of tasks than previously envisaged.[19] Along with an increased focus on international roles, internal roles were both highlighted and given greater attention.[20]

As the examination of evolving internal roles illustrates, they are diverse, dynamic and do not seem to follow a unitary logic even across the very small sample of countries referred to in this paper – countries that reflect similar standards of political and security governance, are operating in a very similar security environment and shared a similar logic during the Cold War. As such, much greater variation is expected if comparative examinations move beyond the context of Western Europe and North America.

Methodological challenges of mapping the armed forces' internal roles

Mapping mostly descriptive information on each of the country case studies (Austria, Belgium, Canada, Denmark, Finland, France, Germany, Italy, Luxembourg, the Netherlands, Norway, Spain, Sweden, the United Kingdom and the United States) enables the gathering of a relatively large amount of information that, if systematically recorded, offers a solid foundation for comparative analysis. Such analyses allow the use of information gathered and lessons learned in one context to compare with and, if suitable, apply in other contexts. This may help in avoiding common mistakes and benefiting from positive experiences in other comparable contexts. Comparative analysis will facilitate an understanding of why and with which consequences certain practices of utilizing armed forces for internal tasks evolved – and if and how these experiences can be relevant to other countries. It also allows for the identification and tracking of trends and emerging norms, particularly if shared across similar political systems and states.

Towards a heuristic framework

A heuristic model developed during background research for this study guides the mapping exercise and analysis presented in this paper.[21] This model (Table 1) provides a matrix to guide a full mapping of internal roles and tasks performed by armed forces.

In addition to mapping evolving non-traditional roles and tasks (beyond national defence), the framework calls for detailed definition and description of the nature of such roles and tasks, and an analysis of their legal basis and legitimacy, as well as the perceived purpose and utility of these functions. The framework asks for information on the specific interests and motivations involved in assigning and fulfilling such tasks and roles to the armed forces, and their impact on issues such as accountability of armed forces, mission objectives, command structures and their "traditional" roles of national defence.

Table 1:   Matrix of non-traditional roles and tasks of the armed forces

Country (Date of analysis)							
Evolving non-traditional roles/tasks (beyond national defence)	Definition and nature of roles/tasks	Legitimacy and legal basis	Purpose and utility for key stakeholders	Interests and motivations of key stake-holders	Impact on account-ability, objectives, command, traditional roles	Competition within security sector*	Threats and opportunities
External/ Inter-national roles/tasks							
Internal/ domestic roles/tasks							
Military roles/tasks							
Civilian/ non-military roles/tasks							
Subsidiary roles/tasks							

*Police, paramilitary forces, private military and security companies and others

Finally, it calls for an analysis of the impact of such new roles on other security institutions – the police, gendarmerie or private security providers – as well as an assessment of the resulting opportunities and threats for both the armed forces themselves and the overall security sector and society at large. This large list of assessment criteria could be applied to internal and external roles, in the context of subsidiary as well as nonsubsidiary functions. The framework could be applied to a wide range of case studies, beyond the geographic scope of this paper.

The mapping and analysis presented in this paper emerged from a much broader mapping typology that focused on a wide range of "non-traditional roles" beyond an armed forces' core task of national defence, including both internal/domestic and external/international roles. Moreover, they were designed to cover a much wider range of explanatory and contextual information on the nature and impact of evolving "non-traditional" roles. A thorough assessment of all these (and possibly additional) criteria is a massive research undertaking – as well as a depth of analysis – that would be beyond the scope of a mostly descriptive and exploratory mapping study. In particular, more comprehensive research would have to rely in large part on "field" research in the countries under study, focusing on the analysis of original documents and local interviews and opinion studies with involved stakeholder communities – conducted ideally by local researchers. Nevertheless, the possibilities arising from applying such a heuristic framework could allow for a more complex analysis of these evolving internal roles, particularly in terms of issues of legitimacy and motivation. The matrix thus offers a glance at how a much broader study of "non-traditional" roles of the armed forces, and possibly all actors within a security sector, can be analysed to advance an increasingly holistic understanding of how a nation's security sector and the relationships, roles and tasks of each actor *vis-à-vis* the others evolve.

The distillation of this framework for the purposes of this paper centres on establishing a clear and usable landscape of the various internal roles performed by armed forces across the countries examined. It is based on a more manageable number of key criteria: a description of a country's political and historical background, as they are of interest for a further analysis of the internal roles of the armed forces; the legal framework for defining (and limiting) such roles; a description of internal roles practised in the particular country; and a brief analysis of those roles compared to those performed by other security institutions – mainly the police, various types of "home guards" and gendarmeries. Comparative findings are based on the results of this mapping exercise.

COMPARATIVE FINDINGS

This section presents the empirical findings of the 15-country review and mapping exercise undertaken for this paper. It begins with a comparative review of internal roles and tasks, followed by a more detailed summary of key tasks – those related to law enforcement, disaster assistance and environmental assistance, various cross-over tasks and miscellaneous community assistance tasks. It concludes with a summary of some common patterns that characterize armed forces' internal roles.

Comparative review of evolving "non-traditional" internal roles and tasks

The study reviews internal roles of armed forces that have emerged and taken place in a number of Western European and North American democracies. It seeks to document and map the range of such roles that are or can be performed by the armed forces of the 15 countries examined. A brief examination is followed by an extensive list of internal roles and tasks observed in the 15 case study countries, enhanced with specific examples. Next, a review of key driving forces behind the armed forces' engagement in these internal roles and tasks is presented, followed by a discussion of preliminary patterns, trends, opportunities and hazards of such evolving roles.

Contrary to popular and traditional conceptions of armed forces' missions, a broad and diverse range of internal roles and tasks are performed by all branches of the armed services in all the countries examined. In fact, some of these tasks are considered core functions of the armed forces according to regulating legal frameworks, such as national constitutions, as well as public organizational mission statements of the armed forces.

Internal roles and tasks of armed forces are varied and increasingly prevalent among the 15 countries examined. The exact role, authority and restrictions depend on historical, legal, social and political contexts that are particular to each country. Typically, internal roles and tasks can include education of civilians (youth re-education centres or specialized training centres); cartographical and meteorological services; road and infrastructure construction, improvement and engineering; and assistance to public administration and the population in case of the occurrence of a major industrial incident, a massive terrorist attack, a sanitary crisis following a major disaster, or natural disasters. They can include search and rescue operations; law enforcement; environmental protection; medical support for poor communities; support of training and education opportunities for disadvantaged youth; border surveillance; provision of security for supplies (food, energy, transport, storage, distribution networks and information systems); security provision during major public events (international sport championships or major global conferences); and the replacement of vital services during work stoppage (strikes or labour movements disrupting economic activity). They can encompass counterterrorism – offensive and defensive measures to prevent, deter or respond to (suspected) terrorist activities; anti-smuggling and anti-trafficking operations; counter-drug operations – detecting and monitoring aerial or maritime transit of illegal drugs; integrating command, control, communications, computer and intelligence assets that are dedicated to interdicting the movement of illegal drugs; supporting drug interdiction and enforcement agencies; and humanitarian aid at home. Many of these tasks are subsidiary ones performed under the command of other security institutions.

For instance, in Belgium these roles and tasks of the armed forces include assistance to the civil population, maintenance of public order and humanitarian assistance and relief assistance in cases of natural disasters and at times of terrorist attacks.[22] In France internal tasks include civil-military actions at home – missions in support of police and gendarmerie; missions to benefit the civilian population and humanitarian missions (the latter can be carried out in cooperation with civilian aid organizations); civil defence – responses to national catastrophes and the preservation of public order; counterterrorism operations; and involvement in other "states of urgency".[23] In Spain the forces provide mostly unarmed civil defence and intervention in cases of emergency and counterterrorism operations.[24] In the UK internal tasks include the restoration of public security, internal emergency and natural disasters.[25] In Canada, upon request, the armed forces provide support during major public events, such as the Olympic Games and international summits, technical and equipment support for enforcement of maritime laws and operations to ensure public order.[26] The Italian armed forces perform a broad range of internal roles and tasks, including operations to restore public order; counterterrorism operations; disaster response, such as combating forest fires; scientific research, including release of meteorological data; and law enforcement.[27] German armed forces handle internal tasks such as support during a state of emergency (e.g. disaster response or restoration of public order); community support, such as harvest support; environmental protection;

Table 2:   Internal roles and specific tasks performed by the armed forces

Law-enforcement-related tasks	Disaster-assistance-related tasks	Environmental-assistance-related tasks	Cross-over tasks	Miscellaneous community assistance
Public order Counterterrorism Border control Drug enforcement Law enforcement Crime investigation Support for major public events Building and personnel security Cyber operations Intelligence gathering	Domestic catastrophe response Disaster relief	Environmental protection	Search and rescue Training Monitoring Equipment and facility provision Miscellaneous maritime activities Scientific research	Examples include colour guard for parades; harvest support

search and rescue missions; and technical aid to assist the police.[28]

The armed forces are thus called upon to assist in internal security provision in situations that require exceptional efforts to respond to exceptional situations – natural or humanitarian catastrophes that exceed civilian and hybrid security institutions' capacities. At the same time, the capacity of civilian security institutions to respond to these situations is kept limited because the situations rarely arise, considerable costs are involved in preparing for them, and these capacities are already maintained regularly by the armed forces and thus exist within easy reach of civilian authorities and security institutions. Thus, under the command and control of civilian agencies, the usually subsidiary operations of the armed forces are designed to enhance the capacity of civilian security providers when assisting in extraordinary internal situations. Table 2 on page 19 presents a broad range of internal roles and specific tasks performed by the armed forces, compiled based on the country research conducted for this paper. The exact duties and responsibilities of the armed forces in the context of each task depend in large part upon the particular scenario and country.

The following paragraphs revisit this list of roles and tasks in more detail, along with examples from the countries covered in the mapping exercise. Figure 1 on page 21 visualizes the distribution of tasks across the 15 countries covered by this study.

Law-enforcement-related tasks

Of the 20 categories of roles identified, ten fall under the broader category of law-enforcement-related tasks. The details of each specific category are provided next. The range of tasks varies substantially in terms of their prevalence across the countries examined and their apparent legitimacy. For instance, this category includes tasks related to "public order" which have been documented in all the countries reviewed. They often appear as one of the core functions of the armed forces as ascribed in the respective constitutions. However, the same category also includes tasks related to "crime investigation", which in contrast have been the least documented, if not most restricted, tasks across the country surveys.

Figure 1:   Distribution of internal tasks

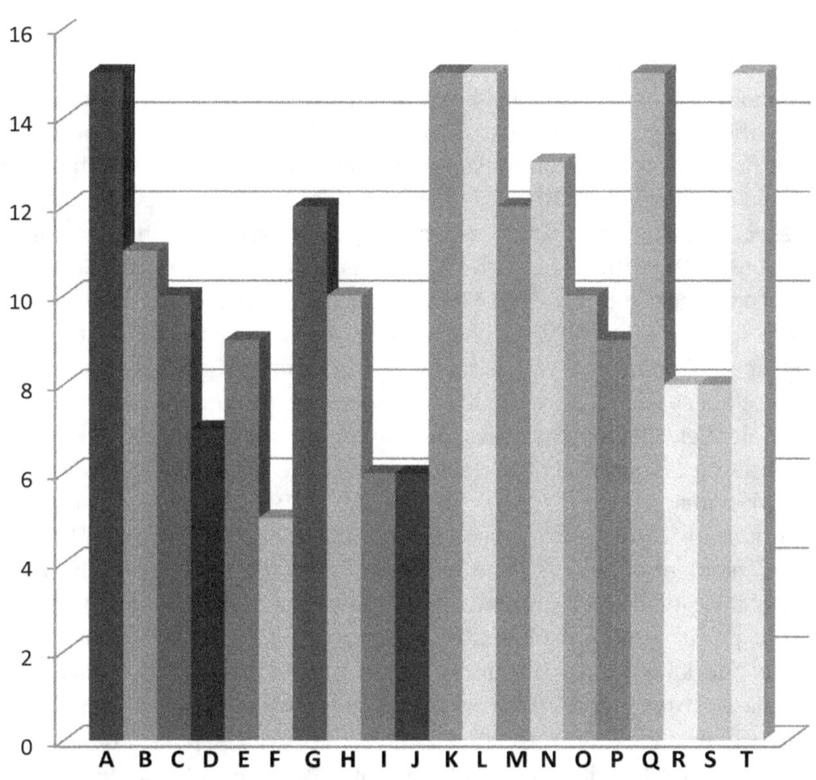

A	Public order	**K**	Domestic catastrophe
B	Counterterrorism	**L**	Disaster relief
C	Border control	**M**	Environmental protection
D	Drug enforcement	**N**	Search & Rescue
E	Law enforcement	**O**	Training
F	Crime investigation	**P**	Monitoring
G	Major public events	**Q**	Equip. & facility provision
H	Building & personnel security	**R**	Misc. maritime activities
I	Cyber operations	**S**	Scientific research
J	Intelligence	**T**	Misc. community assist.

Public order

Public-order-related tasks include support in times of civil disorder and unrest, such as riots, strikes and rebellions. In fact, armed forces of most of the nations in this sample have engaged in public-order-related tasks throughout their history. It has been only relatively recently, for the most part within the past 150 years, that many of the countries examined established certain limits on these types of activities or raised the threshold for their engagement. Often this has coincided with the development of domestic security institutions, especially police services and paramilitary police units. Nonetheless, all the countries surveyed permit their armed forces to engage in public-order-related tasks, which are often referred to as core functions in constitutional and legislative frameworks. Still, such involvement is nearly always limited to situations of last resort or when domestic police services are unable to resolve the threat.

Relatively recent examples of the use of armed forces for public-order-related tasks include the deployment of the Canadian Army against a Mohawk uprising known as the "Oka Crisis" in 1990;[29] and the use of the British armed forces in Northern Ireland, including the notorious "Bloody Sunday" incident of 1972.[30] The 1990 Oka Crisis was a land dispute between the Mohawk indigenous community of Kanesatake and the town of Oka, Quebec, particularly centring on the question of indigenous land rights and historical burial grounds. The dispute escalated to an armed conflict along with massive land and road blockades by protesting members of the Mohawk community. After the deployment of provincial police, followed by the Royal Canadian Mounted Police (RCMP), the Quebec premier invoked section 275 of the National Defence Act to requisition military support in "aid of the civil power". As a result, approximately 2,500 regular and reserve troops were mobilized against the Mohawk militants and protesters, although no shots were fired between them. In the Northern Ireland case, British troops were officially deployed between 1969 and 2007 under the mandate of securing law and order in response to violent tensions between Irish republican and British unionist communities and paramilitary forces during a period known as "the Troubles". The British Army was deployed in support of the Royal Ulster Constabulary and later the Police Service of Northern Ireland, and became a lightning rod for republican forces. It has been estimated that approximately 300 people were killed by British troops during the period, while over 700 British military personnel were killed through the entirety of the Troubles.[31] Legally, much of the deployment fell under the Northern Ireland (Emergency Provisions) Act 1973, which followed the imposition of direct rule of Northern Ireland by the British government. Additionally, in 2002 when the UK firefighters union took industrial action by going on strike, the British armed forces were called into service to provide emergency cover.[32] Troops included firefighters of the Royal Air Force and members of all three branches of the armed forces.

Counterterrorism

Domestic counterterrorism roles have expanded greatly since the terrorist attacks of 11 September 2001. The tasks covered under this label can be vast and vary from state to state. Often they include monitoring external threats to borders, border security, domestic intelligence gathering and post-attack response.

　　While examples of this activity abound, one is French armed forces' deployment as part of Operation Vigipirate.[33] Launched in 1996 and thus pre-dating the 11 September terrorist attacks, over 200,000 French soldiers were deployed under this domestic operation, which was designed to be a permanent security posture.[34] Land, air and sea forces participate in the operation alongside gendarmerie and police, with the purpose of enhancing security and patrols in stations, airports, ports and other key spots; airspace patrol to intercept suspect aircraft; and monitoring maritime activities. Some 1,450 members of the French armed forces are permanently deployed as part of the operation with a particular focus on the Ile de France, the wealthiest and most populated of France's 27 administrative regions and also home to the capital, Paris. In another example, a landmark ruling was made by Germany's highest court in August 2012 reversing long-held restrictions on the internal role of the armed forces by granting permission for them to be deployed as a last resort in states of emergency of catastrophic proportions, including a terrorist attack.[35]

Border control

Border control and surveillance can involve national security, counterterrorism, drug enforcement and immigration enforcement operations. The hybridity of border control depends upon the perceived threats or needs of each country, and can change with time and context.

An example of such activity is also found in the French armed forces. Overlapping with Operation Vigipirate, the French navy provides support to police and gendarmerie forces to interdict undocumented immigrants, smuggling and drug trafficking on the sea.[36] As part of reorganization post 9/11, the Canadian armed forces under Canada Command provide border control support to civil authorities, particularly in terms of counterterrorism checks and prevention of drug smuggling.[37] Recent internal operations of the Italian armed forces include the deployment of 3,000 troops to counter undocumented immigration in 2008. In 2009 troops were deployed to check identities, make arrests and break up illegally erected shelters in Rome.[38]

Drug enforcement

Drug enforcement assistance includes support to local and national police forces and/or gendarmeries in preventing illicit trafficking of controlled substances, particularly at ports of entry, as well as providing assistance, training and equipment for monitoring and arrests. While armed forces of certain states may be more heavily engaged in drug enforcement internationally, for the most part this is more severely limited domestically. However, this engagement allows for cooperation with domestic drug enforcement agencies, such as sharing information and providing technical assistance.

An example is the authorization of US armed forces to support domestic drug enforcement agents.[39] In 1981 the US Congress passed the Military Cooperation with Civilian Law Enforcement Agencies Act to allow military collaboration with civilian law enforcement agencies. Although this Act permits military and civilian law enforcement collaboration on a range of issues, it was particularly designed to combat drug trafficking as part of the burgeoning and so-called "war on drugs".

Law enforcement

Here, the specific task of law enforcement refers to the provision of assistance to facilitate arrests. Assistance may include equipment provision, training and surveillance, but rarely includes personnel to make direct arrests. Indeed, the use of the armed forces for domestic law enforcement remains one of the more controversial internal roles, although eight of the countries surveyed have utilized armed forces to support these efforts. However, tight restrictions are placed upon the direct ability of military personnel to arrest civilians domestically. The US, German and Spanish armed forces hold the strictest prohibition on law enforcement engagement.

Nonetheless, among the many examples illustrating the use of armed forces in supporting law enforcement is the case of Italy, where in 2008 approximately 3,000 Italian military personnel were deployed in support of police patrols to combat crime.[40] Troops were also deployed to embassies and subway and railway stations under the mission of combating violent crime and illegal immigration, although they were not empowered to make arrests directly.[41] In Austria, law enforcement assistance is listed in the country's constitution as one of three core tasks in addition to national defence. In fact, law enforcement assistance can be traced back to the time of the Austro-Hungarian monarchy.[42] The armed forces' engagement in this task must be in response to an official request from civil authorities. According to the constitution, requests are acceptable from law enforcement bodies (e.g. the Ministry of Interior, provincial security directorates, district administration authorities, federal police directorates, mayors and other community entities), criminal courts, state attorneys and criminal and administrative law enforcement authorities. If more than 100 soldiers are needed, the request has to be approved by the federal government.[43] In the case of the Belgian armed forces, which maintain wide latitude in the range of internal tasks they can perform due to minimal constitutional or legal restrictions, law-enforcement-related tasks such as combating organized crime are part of their core mission and considered an aspect of national security.[44]

Crime investigation

Not to be confused with law enforcement, crime investigation-related tasks may include support at crime scenes (e.g. documenting crime scenes and collecting evidence), searching for missing persons and facilitating arrests and/or equipment provision, including surveillance equipment. However, similar to law enforcement tasks, these roles are greatly restricted across the majority of the nations reviewed. Of the roles identified, crime-investigation-related ones were the least cited among the countries surveyed, with just five countries identified as utilizing their armed forces in this way. In particular, tight restrictions are placed on the ability of military personnel to arrest civilians domestically.

Still, authority exists in some of the countries reviewed for armed forces to provide support for crime investigation, such as in Austria, pursuant to Article 79 of the constitution.[45] Likewise, it could be permissible for the Danish armed forces to support crime investigation of civilian security agencies, as there are no constitutional restrictions or prohibitions on their use for internal purposes. Further, the Danish Defence Act[46] sets forth an open-ended range of possibilities. In the US, over three weeks in 2002 two snipers shot and killed ten civilians. Then Secretary of Defense Rumsfeld authorized the use of NORTHCOM in supplying "assets and capabilities", such as aerial surveillance capacities to civilian local and federal law enforcement to track down the snipers.[47]

Support for major public events

Support for major public events varies depending on each event and relevant security agreements made, but can include, among other tasks, providing building and personnel security, air and satellite operations, and medical tents and equipment provision. In addition to global sporting events, such as the Olympics, the relatively recent prevalence of international summits has seen a greater increase in the use of the armed forces in support of domestic security institutions.

Among the many examples are the Canadian Forces' security provision during the 1976 and 2010 Olympics[48] and the French armed forces' security support for the African-France Summit in Nice in 2010.[49] In Canada, under the leadership of the RCMP, the Canadian Forces have been mobilized during the 1976 Montreal Olympics (over 4,500 soldiers), the G8 Summit in Kananaskis in 2002, the Security and Prosperity Partnership meeting in Montebello, Quebec, in 2007 and the 2010 Olympics in Vancouver (4,500 military personnel were mobilized with a budget of $212 million). During the 2010 Vancouver Olympics, security was led by the RCMP but used multiple municipal, provincial and federal agencies, including the Canadian armed forces, deployed as part of Canada Command. The 4,500 military personnel covered land, air and sea capacities, including the use of special operations forces. In addition, the military set up bases and facilities and ran anti-terrorism and biological warfare training exercises, including Operations Bronze, Silver and Gold.[50] Such use of the armed forces to protect major events dates back to the "aid-to-the-civil power" mandate in the 1855 Militia Act. In recent deployments, memoranda of understanding are typically drafted between the RCMP and the Canadian armed forces. In France, as part of the African-France Summit in 2010, approximately 1,200 soldiers and 16 aircraft from the navy and air force were deployed at the request of the prefect of the Alpes-Maritimes.

Building and personnel security

Building and personnel security comprises "physical security measures including guard forces and various surveillance and authentication methods, including biometrics".[51] Often, the armed forces are used to secure royal facilities in constitutional monarchies as well as sites used by foreign dignitaries, particularly embassies, in West European capitals.

Examples include the Belgian armed forces' support of building and personnel security in Brussels.[52] Among other internal roles, such as disaster and domestic catastrophe response, the Military Command of the Brussels Capital Region is prepared to respond to security and crises situations in the region, particularly when the federal police are unable to respond (the Belgian gendarmerie was abolished in 2001). In Italy the armed forces have been used regularly to provide security at identified key sites. For instance, in 2008 1,000 soldiers were sent to guard high-profile public places such as train stations and St Peter's Cathedral in Rome.[53] Finally, in the UK specialized units of the military have been called upon to provide relief, such as during the siege of the Iranian embassy in London in

1980. Commandos from the Special Air Service were deployed to support Scotland Yard police in overcoming the siege and freeing the hostages.[54]

Cyber operations

Cyber attacks involve assaults on computer networks, or exploitation and jamming of equipment. Cyber operations can be offensive or defensive, although they are usually confined to defensive roles in the internal context.[55] In addition, the armed forces may provide technical support and training to domestic agencies or limited sharing of technical equipment.

An example of this is procedures adopted in 2010 in the US that would permit the military to respond to cyber attacks and employ cyber-warfare capabilities following a presidential order and under the control of the Federal Emergency Management Agency. In addition, a memorandum of agreement was signed between the head of the US Department of Homeland Security (DHS) and the Department of Defense in which, among other actions, a team of military networking experts would be assigned to an operations centre of the DHS.[56]

Intelligence gathering

Intelligence gathering refers to domestic data and information gathering. Usually related to another category, such as counterterrorism or drug enforcement, it may also be relevant to general law enforcement and political purposes. However, when used in these two contexts, intelligence-gathering-related activities are often highly restricted in most countries reviewed. Because of the sensitivity of the specific operations, intelligence-gathering tasks tend to be mentioned only vaguely and in passing.

While specific details on the roles and level of engagement of the armed forces in domestic intelligence gathering are quite restricted, such activities are permissible under various pieces of legislation and military operations, such as France's Operation Vigipirate[57] and cooperation between the Military Intelligence Directorate and the Directorate of Territorial Surveillance;[58] or in the form of expanded domestic intelligence gathering by the US military as a result of the US PATRIOT Act.[59] In Norway the armed forces are tasked with providing support for intelligence gathering, justified as an effort "To ensure a good basis for national political and military decision-making through timely surveillance and intelligence. This task comprises surveillance of Norwegian territory and national intelligence. The information is used as basis for the formulation of national policies as well as a prerequisite to solve other tasks like upholding sovereignty, exercising authority, crisis management and collective defence."[60]

Disaster-assistance-related tasks

Two of the 20 identified categories of roles can be grouped under the umbrella of disaster-assistance-related tasks. Of all of the umbrella roles, the use of the armed forces for these tasks appears the least controversial and, increasingly, the most authorized and utilized. Each of the 15 countries reviewed permit the use of its armed forces to provide domestic disaster assistance, although they vary in terms of the triggering mechanisms for deployment.

Domestic catastrophe response

Domestic catastrophe response requires adequate disaster preparedness, including the "[p]lanning, training, preparations and operations relating to responding to the human and environmental effects of a large-scale terrorist attack, the use of weapons of mass destruction" as well as "governmental programs and preparations for continuity of operations (COOP) and continuity of government (COG) in the event of an attack or a disaster".[61] While at times included within concepts, strategies and programmes of "disaster preparedness" or "relief", domestic catastrophe response also exists as its own category, including within military missions and operations.[62] As with disaster-relief-related tasks more generally, domestic catastrophe response represents one of the most prevalent internal uses of the armed forces across the countries surveyed. In addition, it often appears as one of the core tasks of the armed forces as detailed in respective constitutions or core pieces of legislation.

There are many examples of domestic catastrophe response performed by the armed forces. For instance, following contamination of the municipal water supply in Nokia, Finland, affecting roughly 25,500 residents, Finnish armed forces were deployed to secure clean water distribution to local residents in partnership with the Finnish Red Cross and the Volunteer Rescue Service.[63] Following the outbreak of foot and mouth disease in parts of the UK in 2001, the British Army was deployed to contain the outbreak by tracking the contagion and disposing of infected livestock. The troops stayed at local hotels as an attempt to stimulate the local economy.[64] Following the outbreak, the Civil Contingencies Act 2004 was introduced, which made it easier and more efficient for British armed forces to be deployed in times of domestic catastrophe or emergency.[65] Lastly, the armed forces of Luxembourg maintain a chemical, biological, radiological and nuclear unit solely to prepare for responses to domestic catastrophes.[66]

Disaster relief

Disaster relief tasks include efforts to anticipate and respond to natural and man-made disasters (e.g. earthquakes, floods, explosions). This involves preparing for a disaster before it occurs and providing emergency responses, such as evacuation, decontamination and support in rebuilding efforts following a disaster. As noted above, disaster relief is one of the most prevalent internal tasks performed by the armed forces of the countries examined. Like domestic catastrophe response, it often appears as a core military function within national constitutions or key legislation outlining the purpose and scope of the armed forces. This is especially true for the Western European countries examined. Although examples of disaster relief by the armed forces can be found throughout many of the countries' histories, their involvement in these tasks has increased over the past three decades and greater efforts have been made to harmonize and coordinate the armed forces' response with domestic security institutions and other relevant civilian response agencies.

Examples of the deployment of troops for domestic disaster relief include the response to the Red River Floods in Manitoba, Canada (which resulted in over $500 million in damages), when the province of Manitoba requested the deployment of the Canadian armed forces to provide relief to the affected region and help curtail the level of flooding.[67] In Spain, following the Aznalcóllar disaster in 1998 (the rupture of a mine which discharged acidic water, toxic sludge and high concentrations of heavy metals into the surrounding area), the Spanish armed forces were deployed to support the clean-up and evacuation manoeuvres.[68] Some forces have domestic disaster relief inscribed as one of their core functions within relevant legislation, including constitutions. For instance, Article 79 of Austria's constitution specifies disaster recovery as a core task in addition to national defence.[69] As with law enforcement assistance, the provision of disaster relief by Austrian armed forces can be traced back to the Austro-Hungarian monarchy.[70]

Environmental-assistance-related tasks

The third umbrella category, environmental assistance, contains environmental protection as the only group of tasks. Although of course similar to disaster-assistance-related tasks in the context of responses to environmental damage, this category is related specifically to environmental-protection-related tasks.

The role of such protection is aimed at eliminating environmental damage and the degradation of natural resources associated with commercial and recreational activities. Among the examples that illustrate this role are the Italian navy's regular deployment to combat maritime pollution by hydrocarbons and other agents,[71] and the Swedish armed forces support to the 16 domestic environmental quality targets currently established by the Swedish government.[72] According to the Swedish armed forces, "As the concept of ecological sustainability has become more and more accepted, the armed forces decided to focus on the environment and put ecological matters on the agenda when planning their activities … Today integration of environmental work is in progress throughout the armed forces and environmental considerations are an important element of manuals, guidelines, routines, instructions and decisions."[73] Another example is found with the Danish armed forces. As there are no constitutional restrictions on their role, these troops have been able to engage in a wide range of internal roles and tasks, including environmental protection, which falls within their six main functions. In support of civil authorities, Danish armed forces maintain responsibility for state maritime environmental monitoring and maintenance and state maritime pollution control at sea. In addition, they conduct fisheries inspections in the Faroe Islands and Greenland.[74]

Cross-over tasks

The fourth umbrella category for internal functions of armed forces covers "cross-over" tasks. These tasks are grouped together as they relate directly to all three previous umbrella categories: law enforcement, disaster assistance and environmental assistance. During the research it was often difficult to locate precisely the specific umbrella category that these tasks relate to. Further, certain tasks may be performed in the service of law enforcement while at another point and time – or by another country – they are performed in the service of disaster assistance. Thus it deemed appropriate to highlight these cross-over tasks by placing them in a distinct category.

Search and rescue

Search and rescue operations are often performed by a nation's armed forces, aimed at "[m]inimizing the loss of life, injury, property damage or loss by rendering aid to persons in distress and property".[75] While this most commonly covers "humanitarian" actions (e.g. rescuing trapped hikers), it can also relate to law enforcement or armed engagements, such as hostage rescue.

As an example of search and rescue, in 2008 the French military was called upon to evacuate a child with severe heart problems from the island of Corsica.[76] Again, following the crash of an Air France passenger plane in 2009, the French government used the armed forces to assist civil authorities. In particular, a nuclear-powered submarine was deployed to help search for the aircraft's black boxes and over 400 soldiers assisted in the search for and recovery of bodies of those killed in the crash.[77] Such tasks are regularly performed by the French armed forces, and are authorized broadly through the constitution and more specifically detailed in several laws and governmental white papers.[78] In another example from the case studies, the Dutch armed forces regularly provide search and rescue services, such as airlifting patients from ships at sea or the Wadden Islets to hospitals on the mainland.[79]

Training

Training refers to the training provided to law enforcement agents in various relevant tactics and strategies, including use of technology, disruption and use of force. Although it is probable that more than ten of the countries reviewed use their armed forces for training domestic security institutions and government agencies, explicit evidence documenting this role for the remaining five countries was not identified.

Training and information sharing is a regular occurrence between armed forces and other state security institutions. An example is the ongoing training provided by US armed forces to federal and local police.[80] For instance, in 2012 the Los Angeles Police Department held joint military training exercises over four days in part to help "ensure the military's ability to operate in urban environments".[81] Another example is found in Finland. As the Finnish constitution does not restrict the internal roles or tasks of the armed forces, these are articulated for the most part within the Act on the Defence Forces 11.5.2007/551.[82] Section 2 of this Act authorizes the armed forces to provide expert services, including training, to civil authorities for a range of activities, such as rescue operations.

Monitoring

Monitoring includes air and satellite operations related to national defence, disaster preparation, law enforcement and intelligence gathering. In addition, monitoring tasks overlap closely with border control, drug enforcement, counterterrorism, disaster relief and preparedness, and environmental protection.

A prime example of monitoring-related roles is the Norwegian armed forces' ongoing support of surveillance and intelligence operations as part of the national "total defence" doctrine,[83] which is intended to encompass mutual civil-military support and coordination through an entire range of crises and scenarios. For instance, the military may provide monitoring assistance to police on measures such as counterterrorism and disaster preparedness. The Italian armed forces are authorized to perform a range of monitoring-related tasks, particularly as part of disaster preparedness and recovery. This also relates to environmental protection, as they handle various aspects of environmental research at sea, such as water monitoring and exchange of information and data in matters of climatology.[84] As noted earlier, US NORTHCOM provided aerial surveillance assistance to local and federal civilian law enforcement following the shooting deaths of ten civilians in the Washington, DC metropolitan area.[85]

Equipment and facility provision

The provision of equipment and facilities is documented across all the countries examined. It refers to the delivery, lease or operation of technological aid, including vessels, aircraft and facilities for use by law enforcement or other agencies. This represents one of the most common forms of assistance, especially given restrictions on direct involvement in law enforcement.

As examples of equipment and facility provision by armed forces for internal purposes, during the 2006 World Cup the German military supplied material and infrastructure (as well as troops), including triage centres or emergency health provision in key areas. The Danish armed forces are authorized to assist the national hospital system, particularly with equipment and facility support.[86] In Finland, in addition to section 2 of the Act on the Defence Forces, the Act on the Law on Police Tasks in the Armed Forces (3.11.1995/1251)[87] provides further authority for the military to perform internal roles and tasks in support of civil authorities, such as equipment and facility provision. These activities are usually classified as "executive assistance", and 400–500 cases are handled annually by the Finnish armed forces.[88]

Miscellaneous maritime activities

In a number of countries the armed forces perform a range of maritime activities, mainly relating to safety (reducing deaths, injuries and property damage), mobility (facilitating commerce and eliminating interruption of passageways) and certain security elements, such as preventing illegal fishing. Other maritime activities, such as drug enforcement and environmental protection, can be found in specified categories.

For instance, after reports of illegal fishing in its waters, the Canadian navy deployed a submarine to apprehend the *Estai* fishing vessel in 1995.[89] The Swedish armed forces regularly assist the coastguard in collecting and processing maritime traffic.[90] The Royal Netherlands Navy engages in a broad range of maritime activities. According to the navy, "[s]ecurity at sea is essential in order to protect shipping routes and choke-points, both for civilian purposes (such as trade and energy transport) and for military objectives (such as initiating and supporting land operations and carrying out operations at sea)". For these purposes, the navy carries out "patrols and boarding and blockade operations to combat terrorism and prevent gun running and human trafficking", as well as "operations against drug trafficking and piracy)".[91] As a further example, the Danish armed forces are responsible for the National Ice Service, which assists "shipping to and from Danish ports among these the most important supply and export ports, during ice conditions in the Danish waters within the Skaw [cape]".[92]

Scientific research

The armed forces provide a range of scientific and engineering research and development activities, including space research and technology development, cartography and civil engineering projects, such as construction of levees and dams. This group of tasks is one of the more traditional and most consistent internal roles of the armed forces among many of the countries examined.

Examples include the Italian armed forces' regular assessment, collection and dissemination of meteorological data and avalanche risks to the government and the general public.[93] Such activity is authorized generally through Article 52 of the constitution, and specifically in Statute No. 382 of 11 July 1978 on Principles of Military Discipline and Governmental Decree No. 464 of 28 November 1997, Article 5(1), both of which expand the range of authorized internal tasks to be performed by the armed forces.[94] The US Army Corps of Engineers has assisted in building levees and dams as well as cartography of national and local areas for civilian use.[95]

Miscellaneous community assistance

The category of community-assistance-related tasks is the fifth and final identified internal role of the armed forces. Documentation was located among all countries surveyed, and it remains one of the oldest and most

Table 3:　List of internal roles and tasks and countries that are documented or authorized to perform them

Task	Country
Law-enforcement-related tasks	
Public order	Austria, Belgium, Canada, Denmark, Finland, France, Germany, Italy, Luxembourg, Netherlands, Norway, Spain, Sweden, UK, US
Counterterrorism	Austria, Belgium, Canada, Denmark, Finland, France, Germany, Italy, Netherlands, Norway, Sweden, UK, US
Border control	Austria, Belgium, Denmark, Finland, France, Italy, Netherlands, Norway, Sweden, US
Drug enforcement	Austria, Belgium*, Canada, Denmark*, Finland*, France, Germany, Netherlands, Norway*, Sweden*, US
Law enforcement	Austria, Belgium*, Canada, Denmark*, Finland*, France, Italy, Netherlands, Norway*, Sweden*
Crime investigation	Austria, Belgium*, Denmark*, Finland*, France, Netherlands, Norway*, Sweden*, US
Support for major public events	Austria, Belgium, Canada, Denmark, Finland, France, Germany, Italy, Luxembourg, Netherlands, Norway, Spain, Sweden, UK
Building and personnel security	Austria, Belgium, Canada, Denmark, Finland, France, Italy, Netherlands, Norway, Sweden, UK, US
Cyber operations	Belgium*, Denmark*, Finland*, Netherlands, Norway*, Sweden*, UK, US
Intelligence gathering	Belgium*, Denmark*, Finland*, Netherlands, Norway, Sweden*, US

Disaster-assistance-related tasks	
Domestic catastrophe response	Austria, Belgium, Canada, Denmark, Finland, France, Germany, Italy, Luxembourg, Netherlands, Norway, Spain, Sweden, UK, US
Disaster relief	Austria, Belgium, Canada, Denmark, Finland, France, Germany, Italy, Luxembourg, Netherlands, Norway, Spain, Sweden, UK, US
Environmental-assistance-related tasks	Belgium, Canada, Denmark, Finland, France, Italy, Luxembourg, Netherlands, Norway, Sweden, UK, US
Cross-over tasks	
Search and rescue	Austria, Belgium, Canada, Denmark, Finland, France, Germany, Italy, Netherlands, Norway, Sweden, UK, US
Training	Belgium, Canada, Denmark, Finland, France, Germany, Italy, Netherlands, Norway, Sweden, UK, US
Monitoring	Belgium, Canada, Denmark, Finland, France, Germany, Italy, Netherlands, Norway, Sweden, US
Equipment and facility provision	Austria, Belgium, Canada, Denmark, Finland, France, Germany, Italy, Netherlands, Norway, Spain, Sweden, UK, US
Miscellaneous maritime activities	Belgium, Canada, Denmark, Finland, France, Italy, Netherlands, Norway, Sweden, UK, US
Scientific research	Belgium*, Denmark*, Finland*, France, Germany, Italy, Netherlands, Norway*, Sweden*, US
Miscellaneous community assistance	Austria, Belgium, Canada, Denmark, Finland, France, Germany, Italy, Luxembourg, Netherlands, Norway, Spain, Sweden, UK, US

* While affirmative evidence was not identified for the armed forces of these countries to engage in these roles, they are included in this list as there is a lack of explicit legal prohibitions preventing them from engaging in them.
Note: Each country may place varying degrees of restrictions within each role.

consistent internal roles of the armed forces. Community assistance tasks range from harvesting crops to minor community construction projects and providing colour guards for local events, as well as youth outreach and education.

Examples include the German armed forces' support in harvesting or for "aid in social or charitable fields"[96] and the Belgian armed forces' regular engagement in skills-building workshops for youth, vocational courses and fitness training.[97] Likewise, the Swedish armed forces offer courses for civilians within the National Defence College.[98] In addition to a broad range of support provided to civil authorities, the Danish armed forces give assistance to the central customs and tax administration and the hospital system.[99] The Dutch armed forces are authorized to provide support to "social organizations", although this is not viewed as one of their core or priority tasks.[100] Finally, most participation in the armed services is viewed in most countries as useful training for employment in the civil sector. For instance, in Luxembourg the Law from 2 August 1997, amending the Law from 23 July 1952,[101] defines the role of the armed forces in part as offering volunteers a preparation for employment in the public or private sector.

Widely shared reasons behind the armed forces' engagement in internal roles

Through the course of collecting data and mapping the permissible or active internal roles of armed forces in each of the case studies, a number of major driving factors of and motivations for increasingly prominent internal "non-traditional" roles and tasks were identified. Such driving forces naturally vary within each case study in terms of scope and intensity, yet are present throughout all of them.[102] They may be detailed within legislative frameworks guiding and shaping the roles, capacities and purposes of the armed forces, and also emerge from common public reasoning to utilize the armed forces in support or in lieu of civilian domestic security providers.

The first driving factor is the demand to assist the delivery of services normally provided by civilian public services and government agencies which are temporarily unable to do so effectively or adequately. To be sure, across the board the use of the armed forces for internal purposes is only a measure of last resort – and that often in response to exceptional or emergency situations. Thus although the internal roles and tasks identified above have become increasingly prevalent and diverse across the case studies, for the most part they are not conceived as or intended to be central, daily tasks and responsibilities of the armed forces. Instead, civilian domestic security providers are designed to provide a first response and handle the majority of these incidents. Calling on the assistance of the armed forces is considered a measure of last resort, following a request of civilian authorities. Even in the case of maintaining public order or disaster assistance, which may be inscribed in law as a core function of the armed forces, the military becomes involved only when civilian security providers are deemed unable to respond adequately. Likewise, in roles that now have become a regular or "permanent" fixture, such as France's internal deployment of its military under Operation Vigipirate, authorization was considered in response to exceptional needs and circumstances that surpassed the capabilities and resources of the gendarmerie and police.

The second driving factor is the armed forces' comparative advantage in terms of possession of the proper equipment, skills, experience and manpower, as well as unhindered territorial access to all parts of the country. Overwhelmingly, military capacities and resources surpass those of civilian domestic security providers, as the armed forces are structured to provide defence against existential threats to the state and nation, including those that exceed traditionally imagined internal threats. As such, they often maintain and develop skills, training, experience and resources beyond the normal reach of civilian security providers. Certainly, this is relative and varies in each case study, especially considering the vast differences in security and military budgets: in 2011 the US, for example, spent 4.7 per cent of its GDP (approximately US$709 billion) on the military, while Austria spent 0.9 per cent of its GDP (approximately US$3.7 billion) for the same purposes.[103] In regard to equipment and resources, this includes access to everything from satellites to icebreakers, submarines and airlift fleets, as well as financial resources and readily available manpower. The combination of resources, skills and experience suggests that most militaries have a comparative advantage over civilian domestic security providers in these areas, particularly in response to large-scale crises, such as disasters, search and rescue or counterterrorism.

     Albrecht Schnabel and Marc Krupanski

A third driving factor identified in this sample is the ability of the armed forces to serve as a national unifying mechanism that reaches across all communities and classes of society, and all regions of the country, which allows it to impart in citizens a sense of national conscience and patriotism, especially among the youth. This is at times disputed by opponents of military engagement (or proponents of alternative state security providers, such as home or national guards) based on the argument that civilian domestic security providers, such as the police, typically are from the cities, states, provinces or regions in which they are deployed. On the other hand, in various moments of perceived crisis, such as during the firefighter strike in the UK, the mine explosion in Spain or flooding in Austria, militaries are often considered to be imbued with a sense of patriotism and unity, possibly unlike their civilian counterparts. Especially in countries with national conscription, the members of the armed forces include individuals from across the country and service may be viewed as a nationally shared sacrifice and responsibility. Thus the popular support that many militaries receive within consolidated Western democracies makes them favourably situated to engage in internal roles, especially at times of crisis or emergency.

COMPARATIVE ANALYSIS

Overall, contrary to the commonly held perception that armed forces are reserved for national defence against external and traditional military threats, this mapping confirmed that they have been and increasingly are being used for various internal roles and tasks. As contested as this use may be, the military does assist in internal security provision – typically as a resource of last resort in the event of extraordinary situations, such as natural and humanitarian catastrophes and other perceived urgencies that exceed the capacity of civilian and hybrid security institutions.

In addition, certain prominent common traits emerge from the mapping exercise, particularly regarding the armed forces' internal activities related to counterterrorism and disaster assistance. Indeed, the threat of terrorism is an important factor that has recently reshaped the roles of various security institutions (including the armed forces) in several countries. For example, following the terrorist attacks on 11 September 2001, both Canadian and US armed forces established "home commands" with responsibilities over internal territories (Canada Command and NORTHCOM, respectively). Significantly, the creation of Canada Command marked the first time in Canadian history that internal and continental operations of the armed forces are placed under one military commander. Meanwhile, in Germany the role of the armed forces in combating terrorism has been hotly debated since 9/11. For instance, it became evident that German law would make it impossible to stop a civilian airplane from being used as a weapon by shooting it down, as the plane is not a military aircraft and neither the terrorists nor the passengers are officially designated combatants. This and other new factors have led to legal questions and challenges regarding the use of the armed forces. In August 2012 Germany's highest court ruled that the armed forces may be used domestically in cases of extreme emergency and when civilian security providers are incapable of responding adequately.[104]

Through a comparative analysis it is also evident that, although there is a similar trend across countries of an increased domestic counterterrorism role for the armed forces, the exact form in which these roles manifest and operate in relation to other security providers varies significantly across countries. This variation can stem from public opinion, established practices, protocol and legislation, perceived and real threats and capacities. For instance, US authorities have responded to the 11 September attacks by establishing over 1,000 federal agencies, including defence and armed forces branches, charged with intelligence gathering and counterterrorism.[105] On the other hand, European countries for the most part attempt to counter the terrorist threat through established organizations and structures. This carries different implications for the division of mandates, roles and responsibilities – and thus the particular share of domestic security roles – between the armed forces, police and other state security providers, such as gendarmeries.

Factors determining variation in armed forces' internal roles and tasks

Through this mapping exercise ten significant factors have been identified as having an impact on the specific nature of armed forces' internal roles and tasks, while accounting for variation among the case studies. As such, these findings begin to provide some understanding and clarity regarding the roles of armed forces, i.e. their perceived purpose of providing national defence against external threats and their increasing use for internal roles and tasks. Although a much deeper investigation, including field research, utilizing the heuristic framework discussed earlier in this paper could reveal additional factors, the following are believed to be foundational determinants for the degree to which the armed forces of various countries engage in internal roles – and if so, which ones and to what degree (for a summary see Table 4).

Type of political order or system

The first of these factors is the type of political order or system of the country. Although all the countries examined are consolidated democracies, there are different systems of oversight and command of the armed forces between constitutional monarchies and republics. In the cases of constitutional monarchies, the Crown maintains sovereignty over the armed forces and can legally deploy them as seen fit. This is legally the case in countries such as Denmark and the Netherlands. As such, armed forces can conceivably be deployed for any variety of internal roles. On the other hand, in democratic republics such as Germany and the US, the deployment of the armed forces is conceptually more restricted through guiding legislation and parliamentary procedures.

In practice the differences between the two political systems are less pronounced, as the Crown typically delegates its authority to civil government representatives or parliament.

Presence or absence of a constitution

A second factor is the presence or absence of a constitution. As an initial variable the presence of a constitution, or more precisely the absence of one, appears to play an influential part in the degree to which armed forces can engage in internal roles. This factor is for the moment kept separate from questions of restrictiveness within a constitution, which are discussed next. Throughout the case studies, the essential roles, functions and purpose of the armed forces, which set a scope for potential internal activity, are for the most part first established by national constitutions. As a result, any utilization of the armed forces must conform to constitutional principles. Thus it is reasonable that countries without a constitution may have greater flexibility and manoeuvrability in terms of how and where their armed forces are deployed.

Among the case studies, this factor is relevant only for the UK. The UK does not have a single, written constitution and the deployment of armed forces is ultimately a matter of royal prerogative. As a result the UK arguably has had more flexibility to use its armed forces for internal purposes, as they are not constitutionally restricted. Yet restrictions are still found in subsequent legislation. Authorization for internal uses of the armed forces stems mostly from the British tradition of military aid to the civil authorities, an important component of which is the concept of "resilience". "Resilience" is defined in British military terminology as the ability "at every relevant level to detect, prevent, and, if necessary, to handle and recover from disruptive challenges".[106] According to Joint Doctrine Publication 02, published by the Ministry of Defence in September 2007, military support to resilience "is provided at the specific request of the civil authorities, is subject to civil primacy and requires the authorisation of Defence Ministers".[107]

Extent of constitutional restrictions

Closely related to the previous factor is the extent to which constitutions restrict internal use of the armed forces. Although their formation and role tend to be covered in some detail in a country's constitution, the level of explicit restrictions of the armed forces' roles vary greatly. As a result, countries whose constitutions provide little to no restrictions on the use of the armed forces (for internal purposes in particular) enjoy a greater degree of flexibility than those with stricter restrictions. As a country's legal framework is bound by the parameters and rights defined in its constitution, any roles the armed forces take on legally would have to meet those standards.

Countries that put greater constitutional restrictions on their armed forces include Germany, Austria, the US and to a lesser (or at least vaguer) degree Spain. Significantly, as is discussed in the context of subsequent factors, these restrictions were born out of a reaction to counterproductive, possibly destructive, domestic roles played by the armed forces in the past. As such, new constitutions or constitutional amendments attempted to address actual or perceived abuses by the military and restrict its margin of action to prevent their recurrence in the future. In the case of Germany, for instance, at the time of its constitutional convention it had no armed forces and there was no intention to re-establish them, thus they were not reflected in the Grundgesetz (Basic Law). With the reintroduction of the armed forces, the Basic Law had to be amended carefully, strict prohibitions were set on the ability of the armed forces to engage in domestic activities, and clear divisions were established between the police and the military.[108] Articles 35 and 91 demarcate the domestic roles that the armed forces are allowed to carry out, in times of great emergency or catastrophe and conducted in a subsidiary role to civilian security providers.[109]

On the other hand, a number of countries examined do not include significant explicit restrictions on the roles of the armed forces within their constitutions. This allows a greater variety of roles, including internal ones, to be taken on by the armed forces. Among the case studies that demonstrate this feature are Belgium and Norway. The only constitutional restrictions in Belgium are that its armed forces cannot contravene international law of war. For Norway, few restrictions are outlined in the constitution, allowing for the development and application of the "total defence" concept and the active use of the Home Guard for a variety of purposes. Indeed, the central restriction to its internal roles is found in Article 99 of the constitution, which insists that that no one may be taken into custody except in cases determined by law. The government is also not authorized to employ military force against its citizens, "except in accordance with the forms prescribed by law, unless any assembly disturbs the public peace and does not immediately disperse after the Articles of the Statute Book relating to riots have been read out clearly three times by the civil authority".[110]

Historical context

A fourth significant factor is a country's particular historical context (such as an authoritarian past) immediately preceding the foundation of the current political system and constitution. Often influencing the previous factor of explicit constitutional restrictions on the roles of armed forces, a perceived negative historical context involving the armed forces is an additional factor that shapes whether, in what ways and to what extent a country utilizes its military for internal purposes. In the cases of the consolidated democracies examined here, those with a recent authoritarian past or heavy military presence domestically face greater restrictions on their internal roles and tasks.

Prime examples of this include Germany, Austria and, to some extent, Spain. Certainly, the experiences of Nazism and the Second World War resulted in considerable restrictions upon the armed forces' ability to engage in internal tasks. As seen in the case of Germany, and many other countries in this survey, the roles and tasks of the armed forces, particularly internal ones, are clearly noted in the constitution in order to prevent a return to their authoritarian and militarist past. For instance, Spain's military has a long history of engagement in internal affairs. Although General Franco's militarist rule ended in 1976 and a new constitution was drafted in 1978, shepherding a process of democratization, true and effective civilian control of the military did not materialize until 1996. The November 1996 decision to join NATO's military structures forced significant modernization and reform of the military. Until this point, Spanish soldiers had refused to accept civilian and democratic control, attempted a *coup d'état* in 1982 and only swore allegiance to the Crown. By 1996, however, "soldiers finally began to accept it [civilian control] and did not choose to collectively express their discomfort at their diminished position".[111] Although there is debate as to which internal roles of the armed forces are precisely permitted by the constitution, it is explicit that any internal roles must be unarmed.

Military history

Fifth, a slight variation of the previous factor is more broadly a country's military history, such as a colonial past or recent experience with internal or international war. The memories and legacies of this past strongly influence the development of the armed forces' internal roles, the division of tasks between them and other security institutions, and the creation and interpretation of corresponding legal frameworks.

There are numerous examples among the case studies to illustrate the validity of this factor. One of the most prominent is found in the case of the US. For instance, the US Civil War and the post-war reconstruction period left significant imprints upon the role of the US armed forces in internal affairs. After 11 southern US states declared secession, the Civil War, which lasted from 1861 to 1865, divided the country between the North and the South. The war was the bloodiest in US history, with over 600,000 soldiers killed along with an untold number of civilian casualties. After the North's victory the country entered a period known as "reconstruction", which lasted until the "Compromise of 1877".[112] During this time the US Army occupied the southern states, which increasingly bred resentment. As a key element of the Compromise of 1877, the US federal government agreed to withdraw its troops from the southern states. It subsequently passed the Posse Comitatus Act of 1878, which prohibits US armed forces from directly enforcing domestic law. This move served to counter fears that the army would become a national police force.

On the other hand, the historical experiences of occupation during the Second World War have prompted Denmark, the Netherlands, Finland and Norway to allow for greater leeway in terms of the internal roles their armed forces are permitted to play. Indeed, these experiences encouraged the desire for strong and independent military forces not just to prevent future invasion or occupation, but also to respond to any crisis or catastrophe on domestic soil. Finland and Norway have developed concepts of "total defence", according to which their militaries are designed to respond effectively and appropriately to any perceived or real threat, whether this falls under disaster assistance, counterterrorism or maintenance of public order. This resulted in fewer and less explicit constitutional restrictions on the roles of the armed forces, as compared to those in Germany, Austria or the US, for instance.

Presence of gendarmeries or home guards

The sixth factor is the presence of gendarmeries or home guards, which are technically not part of the armed forces. The presence of hybrid police-military institutions, such as a gendarmerie, can lessen the demand and perceived need for armed forces to assume internal roles, especially those related to law enforcement. It can also increase the threshold of tasks for which their assistance is requested, as they will not be involved as long as the hybrid institution is able to manage the situation. In some circumstances the presence of a hybrid organization may make it more likely that the armed forces play a subsidiary role to that organization, once they are asked to become involved.

Examples illustrating this factor include Spain (Guardia Civil), France (Gendarmerie), Italy (Carabinieri), Sweden (Hemvärnet) and, to a certain degree, Canada (RCMP) and the US (National Guard). For instance, the Spanish Guardia Civil is tasked with a wide variety of security roles, including the maintenance of public order; prevention and investigation of crimes; prevention of criminal acts; ensuring the safety of goods and persons; law enforcement; protection of public buildings and installations; collaboration with civil protection units in cases of grave risks, catastrophes or disasters; counter-trafficking activities; ensuring the security of various infrastructure and communication networks, ports, airports and borders; inter-city transportation of prisoners; and the protection of natural resources.[113] France provides for the National Gendarmerie to be deployed in missions abroad, and at home it allows the gendarmerie to ensure public order, especially in rural areas, to gather information and intelligence on counterterrorism and to ensure the protection of the country's nuclear armament.[114] Gendarmeries in particular have been created precisely because certain challenges require more than the police can offer, but less than a military response would entail. In the case of Canada, many internal tasks performed by the armed forces, such as support during major international events or law enforcement, are generally done in a subsidiary and support role to the RCMP. All these institutions provide considerable domestic services that arguably lessen the need for the armed forces to engage in internal roles, especially when it comes to law enforcement. Additionally, they can serve to circumnavigate restrictions on the use of the armed forces domestically, such as in the case of the US National Guard, and to provide readily available military assistance domestically.

Presence of services within the armed forces with explicit internal roles

Seventh, a further factor influencing whether or not – and in which ways – the armed forces assume internal roles is the presence of services within the forces that are specifically authorized and assigned to engage in internal roles. This may seem an obvious point, but bears explicit mention nonetheless. Unlike gendarmeries or home guards that are organizationally or legally external to the military, some of the countries examined maintain entire branches or select units within their armed forces with the authority and mission to provide internal roles. The existence of such branches or units increases the likelihood of active involvement in internal roles as well as the possible variety of those roles.

Among the examples found in the case studies is the role of the US Coast Guard. Although part of the US armed forces, the Coast Guard is expressly authorized to conduct law enforcement and crime investigation tasks, in addition to other internal roles such as drug enforcement, border control, search and rescue and disaster assistance. As a means to account and reflect this differentiation, the Coast Guard is not a component of the Department of Defense, as are the other four branches of the armed forces. It belongs to the Department of Homeland Security (and formerly the Department of Transportation). Thus the Coast Guard is not only regularly engaged in internal roles and tasks, but these form the majority of its activities.

The Heimevernet (Home Guard), which is part of the Norwegian armed forces, forms the core of territorial and internal defence in times of peace, crisis and armed conflict. Founded in 1946, the Home Guard has its origins in the resistance movement of the Second World War. Today it has approximately 50,000 personnel. Its current structure is divided into three components: army (80 per cent), navy (10 per cent) and air force (10 per cent).[115] In addition it maintains specific units, such as the Rapid Reaction Force and Follow-on Force, tasked with force protection, counterterrorism and securing critical infrastructure sites, among other responsibilities.

External determinants

An eighth factor contributing to variation among the countries examined relates to external determinants. They include geographical conditions, industrial assets and geographic proximity to and borders with regions and countries that have a strong impact on the state's and population's perceived and real threats, risks and needs. Certainly, each country possesses unique characteristics and resources that help shape and inform its determined internal and external security needs and priorities – and the perceived needs for the armed forces to play a role in securing them.

For instance, because of its maritime boundaries, the Netherlands armed forces are frequently used internally for environmental protection, search and rescue and disaster response. Moreover, security delivered from the sea is usually needed in support of combat activities on land (ammunition, food, water, providing medical and humanitarian assistance, gathering and supplying intelligence and providing fire support). National maritime tasks are deemed to be of vital national and public importance, and involve activities such as coastguard and search and rescue missions, combating terrorism, clearing unexploded mines and bombs, providing diver assistance and medical assistance to divers, carrying out hydrographical surveys and supporting civil authorities in dealing with natural disasters.[116]

In addition to support for maritime activities like the Dutch, the Italian and French armed forces provide domestic support for mountain rescues and periodical bulletins on Alpine avalanche risks, as well as responses to forest fires.[117] Beyond supporting maritime-related activities, under the Canada First Defence Strategy the Canadian armed forces have taken an increasingly large role in patrolling, monitoring and securing the Canadian Arctic region.[118]

Recent or ongoing internal conflicts

Another key factor to explain variation among the case studies is a country's experience of recent or ongoing internal conflicts and disputes. In cases of active armed conflicts or disputes within the boundaries of a national territory, the armed forces of most countries would be engaged. Typically, police services and hybrid security institutions, such as gendarmeries, are called upon as an initial security provider. However, if the threat is deemed exceptional or enduring, the armed forces of most of the countries reviewed would be deployed in an attempt to contain and eliminate the threat.

An example of this, discussed in a previous section, is the deployment of UK armed forces to Northern Ireland to contain violence, initially between republican and unionist factions and paramilitaries and later in their confrontation with the Irish Republican Army. Not only does this serve as an example of the armed forces' role in this conflict, but it also established legal precedents on which the government has attempted to base subsequent policies, particularly regarding counterterrorism.

Membership in military alliances or regional bodies

The tenth and final factor identified is a country's membership in military alliances or regional frameworks and bodies. Membership in any of these may either place certain limitations on the roles the armed forces can undertake domestically or require certain minimum levels of military preparedness that, absent an external threat, may be utilized in a subsidiary role in support of civil domestic security providers.

Table 4:　Factors accounting for variation among countries examined and examples

Factor	Example
Type of political order or system	Constitutional monarchies (e.g. Denmark,Netherlands) versus democratic republics (e.g. Germany, US)
Presence or absence of a constitution	Absence (e.g. UK)
Extent of constitutional restrictions	Relatively greater constitutional restrictions (e.g. Austria, Germany, Spain, US) versus relatively no constitutional restrictions (e.g. Belgium, Finland, Norway)
Historical context	Relatively recent experience with authoritarianism or militarism domestically (e.g. Austria, Germany, Spain)
Military history	Perceived relatively positive experiences with armed forces' internal deployment or experience of foreign occupation (e.g. Denmark, Finland, Netherlands, Norway) versus perceived relatively negative experiences with internal deployment (e.g. US)
Presence of gendarmeries or home guards	Presence of hybrid police-military services (e.g. Canada, France, Italy, Spain, Sweden, US)
Presence of services within the armed forces with explicit internal roles	Includes specialized units (counterterrorism units), dedicated branches (e.g. armed forces "home guard" units) or branches with internal jurisdiction (e.g. coastguard) (e.g. Canada, Norway, US)
External determinants	Includes issues such as geographical conditions (e.g. mountainous regions or maritime zones) and industrial assets (e.g. nuclear facilities) (e.g. Austria, Canada, Denmark, France, Italy, Netherlands, UK, US)
Recent or ongoing internal conflicts	Recent experience with internal armed conflict necessitating armed forces' engagement (e.g. UK)
Membership in military alliances or regional bodies	Could have a push or pull factor – i.e. requiring higher readiness and capacity on particular measures or allowing for lower national defence resourcing due to alliances, such as NATO or European Defence Community (e.g. Luxembourg)

For instance, Luxembourg's membership in NATO, the Treaty of Brussels and the European Defence Community lessens its need to prepare for "total defence" against external security threats. As a result, it also lessens the resources the armed forces have to utilize for internal purposes in addition to investing in civilian security providers. This in part echoes the "free loader" argument that by virtue of joining a security alliance, some members may feel less pressured to invest in military preparedness or contribute military assets and resources to the alliance.

Common traits across the case studies

In addition to key factors explaining variation of roles and tasks among the case studies' armed forces, there are three common traits that emerge from the mapping exercise (see Table 5 for a summary).

The first of these traits is found in the samples analysed for this study and in line with common knowledge: the armed forces are not the primary domestic security providers within a country's security sector. They are secondary security providers that are called upon under exceptional circumstances, when police or gendarmeries are not in a position to respond adequately to a particular security challenge.

For each country examined, alternative civilian domestic security providers exist, such as the police (including local and federal), gendarmerie and border patrol. They are designed for and usually capable of providing the range of domestic roles and tasks described in more detail earlier in this paper. However, either under legislation detailing their roles or common law and practice, the armed forces may be called upon to provide assistance to their civilian domestic counterparts in times of declared emergency or catastrophe. Of course, the exact definition or threshold of what constitutes an emergency varies across the countries and often remains contested. Nonetheless, this trait remains true.

An example of this option of last resort, particularly in a subsidiary role, is the Canadian armed forces' support of domestic law enforcement, including provincial police and the RCMP. Often, in order to engage the armed forces' support in specific domestic cases, a memorandum of understanding (MOU) is drafted and signed between the relevant armed forces component and the domestic agency requesting support (e.g. RCMP, provincial government or a federal department). For example, an MOU exists between the Department of National Defence and the Department of Fisheries and Oceans Canada to authorize and engage the Canadian Navy as an "active participant in fisheries enforcement". Additionally, an MOU was drafted between various agencies, including the armed forces, to provide security during the 2010 Winter Olympics in Vancouver. The MOU authorized the use of 4,500 military personnel in land, air and sea capacities and allocated $212 million of the total security budget to the armed forces.[119]

Indeed, according to Public Safety Canada's website, "Emergencies are managed first at the local level: hospitals, fire departments, police and municipalities. If they need assistance at the local level, they request it from the provinces or territories. If the emergency escalates beyond their capabilities, the provinces or territories seek assistance from the federal government. The coordination and provisioning of resources can move quickly from the local to the national level."[120]

In the case of Finland, the Act on the Defence Forces details that the armed forces are authorized to provide "support for other authorities, including the following: a) executive assistance to maintain public order and security, to prevent and interrupt terrorist acts and otherwise to protect society at large; [and] b) assistance in rescue operations by contributing equipment, personnel and expert services".[121]

According to Article 91 GG of the German Basic Law, there are three prerequisites for the armed forces to be deployed in cases of internal states of emergency: imminent danger to the existence or the free democratic basic order of the federation or a state; the endangered state/s is/are not able or willing to combat the danger; and the police and the border guards are not enough to fight off the danger. Hence, the armed forces are the option of last resort and strictly subsidiary.[122]

As a second common trait that emerges across the case studies, every country is involved in the provision of aid with the help of armed forces in cases of natural or humanitarian disasters. This is largely undisputed and accepted across broad political spectrums, among the political elites as well as the general public.

For example, following massive snowfalls that resulted in severe flooding in Lower Austrian villages along the Morava River, more than 550 Austrian soldiers were deployed, with technical support, to stem the flooding and supply food and daily items to affected communities.[123] Some countries, such as Denmark, have established specialized agencies within their ministries of defence to prepare and respond to these threats. For instance, the Danish Ministry of Defence oversees the Danish Emergency Management Agency, which "[p]rovides assistance to local emergency

Table 5:   **Common traits across the case studies and examples**

Trait	Examples
The armed forces are not the primary internal security providers within a country's security sector; they are secondary security providers that are called upon under exceptional circumstances, when police or gendarmeries are not in a position to respond adequately to a particular security challenge	Support of Canadian armed forces to Department of Fisheries and Oceans Canada in fisheries enforcement Finnish Act on Defence Forces detailing subsidiary last resort and upon request role German Basic Law, Article 91 GG, articulating three prerequisites for armed forces deployment (imminent existential danger; inability of civil authorities to contain danger; inability of civil security providers to contain danger)
Every country is involved in provision of aid with the help of armed forces in cases of natural or humanitarian disasters or domestic catastrophes	Deployment of 550 Austrian soldiers after flooding of Morava River Development of Danish Emergency Management Agency within Ministry of Defence UK armed forces' deployment to contain the spread of foot and mouth disease
Increasing domestic counterterrorism roles performed by armed forces	Formation of Canada Command in 2006 includes use of Canadian armed forces to respond to terrorist threats France's Operation Vigipirate has deployed over 200,000 armed forces since 1996 Development and engagement of US Defense Intelligence Agency and NORTHCOM

management, police, and other authorities in the event of major or longer-lasting emergency efforts; [p]rovides assistance in the event of international natural or man-generated disasters; [s]upervises and counsels local emergency management agencies; and [c]oordinates emergency management planning in the civilian sector".[124]

Lastly, as the third common trait among the case studies the threat of terrorism is an important factor that has recently reshaped the roles of various security institutions (including the armed forces). A similar trend has been emerging across countries in terms of an increased domestic counterterrorism role for the armed forces. The exact form in which these roles manifest and operate in relation to other security providers varies significantly, depending on public opinion, established practices, protocol and legislation, perceived and real threats and capacities.

Prime examples are France's previously discussed Operation Vigipirate as well as the engagement of US armed forces and reorganization of the Canadian armed forces. For the US military, domestic counterterrorism roles have vastly expanded since 11 September 2001 to include monitoring external threats to borders, border security, domestic intelligence gathering and post-attack response. There are over 3,000 government and private organizations specializing in counterterrorism, including many components of the armed forces, such as the Office of Naval Intelligence, Defense Intelligence Agency and NORTHCOM homeland command. In the post-9/11 environment, a greater and more concentrated effort has taken place to consolidate a domestic military command and be better able to engage in internal affairs. On 1 February 2006 Canada Command was established, to be "responsible for the day-to-day oversight of domestic and continental routine and contingency Canadian Forces operations. In the conduct of domestic operations, the command also coordinates, when requested, military support to Canadian civil and law enforcement authorities." It helps "anticipate and respond to potential threats to Canada and Canadians".[125]

Potential hazards and opportunities of armed forces' involvement in internal roles and tasks

The mapping exercise revealed a number of hazards and opportunities related to the armed forces' involvement in internal roles and tasks. While all of these may not yet have empirical documentation, they stand as potential prognoses and forecasts that should be taken into consideration when conducting further analysis on the contemporary evolution of armed forces' relationship to internal roles and tasks.

Hazards

Hazards of granting the armed forces a more prominent internal role may include fear of losing civilian control over the forces and the military establishment's potential assertion of a greater role and influence in society and politics, thus eroding the principle of separating civilian and military authority.[126] There is also fear about creeping militarization of civilian technical tasks, civilian partners in subsidiary missions and the population overall, and the militarization of genuine policing tasks of the justice system and penal institutions. Finally, there are fears about potential misconduct and abuse by the armed forces due to improper training for internal deployment and inadequate understanding of applicable civil and criminal law and procedures. On the part of the armed forces, inadequate special training on internal roles does little to address the potential lack of local understanding and sensitivities required to respond effectively to local crises or needs. Finally, investing in the armed forces' dual internal and external roles might happen at the expense of public finances and adequate personnel levels among civilian institutions.

Similar to expanding the armed forces' international roles, strengthening their domestic footprint also raises the risks of eroding preparedness for core functions of national defence and war-fighting abilities.[127]

Opportunities

In contrast, a number of *opportunities* may arise from expansion of the armed forces' internal roles and tasks. They include the provision of important peacetime contributions to the safety and security of society, and the ability to resolve national crises (e.g. natural disasters or widespread civil disturbances) that could otherwise not be resolved with civil means and instruments alone. It allows the deterrence of non-state armed challengers to domestic and regional security and stability through the maintenance of an independent domestic capacity to respond to threats. Particularly when circumstances necessitate heavy weaponry or specialized technology, utilizing the armed forces to deliver these could help prevent heightened militarization of regular domestic security forces and trigger greater public and legal scrutiny of their use. Finally, as an organizational interest, the addition of internal roles and tasks may develop new areas of expertise and (budgetary) relevance of armed forces at a time when traditional external military threats are considered to be low.

CONCLUSION

There are a number of direct benefits of mapping the internal and other "non-traditional" roles of a country's armed forces. First, comparing roles with counterparts in other countries heightens awareness of the political and historical reasons for particular roles assigned to one's armed forces. It also reveals the demands and limits put on the armed forces in responding to domestic security needs.

Second, tracking and assessing evolving roles over time sharpen awareness of the armed forces' changing place and function in society as a security provider. A basic mapping of roles and tasks will reveal the evolution towards more or perhaps less involvement in domestic security provision, depending also on the evolving roles and capacities of civilian security institutions, such as the police, gendarmeries or disaster management mechanisms. More comprehensive mapping exercises that search for additional information, as suggested by the heuristic framework presented earlier in the paper (see Table 1), would generate further, potentially revealing and useful information on evolving public opinion, and point to evolving attitudes and organizational responses by security institutions in terms of capacity, structure, training and equipment, as well experiences with subsidiary engagements.

Third, thorough and systematic analyses of the changing historical, legal, political, economic, social and environmental contexts of the armed forces' internal roles and tasks over time sensitize and sharpen the military's awareness of the contexts in which internal roles are defined and applied.

Mapping and analysing evolving internal (and other "non-traditional") roles of the armed forces generate practical information on best practice for cooperation and subsidiary collaboration between different security institutions. Updated information is produced on divisions of tasks and responsibilities between police, gendarmerie, military and other domestic security providers, based on an informed understanding of respective roles and tasks. Such data can be used to inform organizational and budgetary planning across the security sector and within individual institutions. Producing those assessments and planning jointly between the armed forces and other security institutions, including governmental and non-governmental oversight bodies, represents best practice in holistic security sector planning. Security-providing institutions and their external management and oversight institutions would then be able to assess and assure that evolving roles – also *vis-à-vis* or in collaboration with other security institutions – are adequately reflected in training and education. Additionally, this could assist policy-makers in understanding how legislation and other governance mechanisms of the roles and tasks of armed forces may develop and evolve. Finally, appropriate efforts can be made to ensure that subsidiary and joint roles are supported with common training, planning and evaluation among different institutions. This may lead to greater cooperation and synchronization among security providers, which in turn would improve effectiveness, efficiency and governance.

Analysing information collected with the help of a structured typology triggers further enquiries into contradictions and inconsistencies that are created within a nation's security sector in relation to evolving separations and overlaps of tasks, competencies, responsibilities and authorities. Useful lessons can be learned from countries where such shifts have taken place and the armed forces, other security institutions, the state and society had to adapt to those new challenges. New competencies had to be developed, others had to be dropped. Particularly in such evolving contexts, the armed forces and other security institutions have to embrace new "non-traditional" roles while maintaining a sensible level of capacity and preparedness to face "traditional" threats. Defence reform programmes, for instance, focusing on the armed forces and ideally pursued in the context of larger security sector reform programmes, are ultimately driven by such political and societal changes, along with evolving internal and external security environments. In established as well as transforming security sectors (in preparation for or during reform processes) it is crucial that additional roles for the armed forces are accommodated in terms of accountability (such as civilian oversight) and internal command structures. Tracking public support of or opposition to changing and new roles and tasks of the armed forces can inform communication strategies that are crucial ingredients of ultimately successful and sustainable reform processes.

A further advantage of systematic and thorough tracking of changing roles relates to the utility and necessity to keep abreast of such dynamics in transforming environments, for instance in the context of fragile and post-conflict societies. This means that the specific questions asked in the context of the heuristic framework presented in this paper need to be adapted for charting and analysing the existing and evolving roles of armed forces in countries outside this particular sample of West European and North American established democracies. Once adjusted, the findings could be of significant value to those states (and relevant security sectors) as they are in the process of redefining and recalibrating the roles of their armed forces – and, by necessity, the entire security sector – in response to evolving societal needs and new internal and external security realities.

There is also much to be gained from mapping and tracking armed forces' evolving roles in other countries – with comparable as well as different historical, political or legal contexts. Comparison with other countries' approaches to and experiences with internal roles of the armed forces raises awareness of comparative advantages of the military, particularly *vis-à-vis* the option of bolstering the capacities of civilian security providers and crisis and disaster management bodies to meet domestic security needs. Such comparisons can serve as the basis for considering potential financial implications, based on other countries' experiences. They also offer best practice suggestions for avoiding redundancies and duplications across different security institutions and making collaborative cross-security-sector approaches work. Looking at other countries can help with uncertainties about appropriate organizational decisions if there is a risk that too many authorities with similar competencies create unclear organizational structures and overlapping or competing competencies and capacities, ultimately resulting in rifts between diverse and competing domestic security institutions. A holistic approach to security sector governance is meant to prevent such problems. Thus joint mapping and planning of roles and tasks is an important activity within good security sector governance.[128]

This paper has examined a substantial empirical body of evidence revealing that armed forces are increasingly assuming internal roles and tasks along with their traditionally assumed role and function within the Western paradigm to provide national defence against traditional external security threats. To probe, document and make sense of this reality, the paper has examined armed forces' internal roles in a variety of consolidated Western democracies. In this context the study undertook a mapping exercise covering 15 countries: Austria, Belgium, Canada, Denmark, Finland, France, Germany, Italy, Luxembourg, Netherlands, Norway, Spain, Sweden, the United Kingdom and the United States of America.

The mapping exercise generated information on the types of internal roles and tasks performed by armed forces in these countries, and the political and legal contexts in which these roles evolved. A comparative analysis of the results of this exercise generated a number of initial lessons and patterns. It also highlighted important issues and questions that merit further analysis, drawing on the initial framework discussed and applied in this paper.

The armed forces surveyed assist in internal security provision as a resource of last resort in circumstances that require efforts to respond to exceptional situations. These include natural and humanitarian catastrophes and other urgencies that exceed the capacity of civilian and hybrid security institutions. In addition, subsidiary operations under the command and control of civilian agencies are designed to enhance the capacity of civilian security providers in such situations.

A variety of internal roles and specific tasks of the armed forces have been documented in this paper. They include:

- law-enforcement-related tasks, including public order, counterterrorism, border control, drug enforcement, law enforcement, crime investigation, support for major public events, building and personnel security, cyber operations and intelligence gathering

- disaster-assistance-related tasks, including domestic catastrophe response and disaster relief
- environmental-assistance-related tasks, including environmental protection
- cross-over tasks, including search and rescue, training, monitoring, equipment and facility provision, miscellaneous maritime activities and scientific research
- various miscellaneous community assistance tasks.

Further, based upon a comparison of the 15 case studies, ten factors are identified as having an impact on the specific nature of armed forces' internal roles and tasks.

- Type of political order or system.
- Presence or absence of a constitution.
- Constitutional restrictions on the roles of armed forces.
- Historical context (such as authoritarian past) immediately preceding the foundation of the current political system and/or constitution (or the equivalent).
- Historical past (e.g. colonial past, experience of recent war) with strong influence on the development of the internal roles of the armed forces, the division of tasks between armed forces and other security institutions, and corresponding legal frameworks.
- Experiences with gendarmeries or home guards.
- External determinants such as geographic conditions, industrial assets and geographic proximity to and borders with regions and countries with a strong impact on the state's and population's perceived and real threats, risks and needs.
- The presence of services within the armed forces that are specifically privileged with engagement in internal roles.
- Recent or ongoing internal conflicts and disputes.
- Membership in military alliances or regional frameworks and bodies.

A number of common traits emerged from the mapping exercise across the 15 case studies. *First*, in the samples analysed and in line with common understandings, the armed forces are not the primary domestic security providers within a country's security sector. They are secondary security providers called upon under exceptional circumstances, when police or gendarmeries are not in a position to respond adequately to a particular challenge. *Second*, every country in this study utilizes its armed forces in cases of natural disaster. This is largely undisputed and accepted across broad political spectrums, among elites as well as the wider public. *Third*, the threat of terrorism is an important factor that has recently reshaped the roles of various security institutions (including the armed forces) in several countries. Across countries there is an increased domestic counterterrorism role for the armed forces. The exact form in which these roles manifest and operate in relation to other security providers varies significantly: it depends on public opinion, established practices, protocol and legislation, and perceived and real threats and capacities.

Relatively recent political and in some cases historical events are shaping not only the roles but also the "traditional" place of the armed forces in their societies. Societies in many parts of the world are faced with the daily reality or risk of violent conflict. It is therefore understandable that different opinions exist in many of the countries covered in this paper on the necessity to retain a fighting force that is ready to defend society from external or internal military attacks. For the countries reviewed here – with the exception of terrorist activities – the core function of national defence has lost significance. The risk of external military aggression is diminishing in the perception of the population and their political representatives. The latter are therefore, for the most part, less willing to spend public resources to prepare for seemingly remote threats.

These views might be unique to societies that have, at least since the end of the Second World War, experienced an unprecedented level of peace and stability at home and in their immediate neighbourhood. This remains true even though this sense of security rested on very unstable grounds during the Cold War and was challenged in different ways during the explosion of ethnic violence in the wake of the Yugoslav successor wars in their immediate backyard – and more recently across the Mediterranean Sea throughout Northern Africa.

In addition to external instability and violence, one event in particular has sensitized post-Cold War societies in the global North to the continuing possibility of armed attacks on their own populations and soil: the terrorist attacks of 11 September 2001 in New York, followed soon after by further bombs in Madrid and London. These were not major attacks in historically

                    Albrecht Schnabel and Marc Krupanski

relative terms of human casualties and infrastructure damage. But they did have a psychologically powerful impact on the psyche of previously safe populations. The response was the proclamation of a so-called "war on terror" which has mobilized support for the retention and in some cases even expansion of armed forces to take on very "traditional" defence tasks.

Military engagements in places such as Afghanistan, Iraq or Libya – and calls for military support to political protest movements against authoritarian leaders throughout the Arab world – have reignited sensitivities about "traditional" combat requirements. In addition, the crises, human suffering, economic damage and political instability created by natural disasters point to an increasing demand for the involvement of the armed forces in facilitating immediate responses to such crises. Modern armed forces are increasingly called upon to expand dual- or multiple-role capacities that allow them to address both "traditional" and "non-traditional" threats. The latter could in some cases become their primary roles.

However, changes in the armed forces' *raison d'etre* (and the division of roles and tasks among all security institutions within society) need to be made carefully. This should always follow a thorough assessment of potentially emerging threat scenarios. The threats for which security sectors were put in place, trained and equipped might be changing. This applies to countries in the North as in the South. This study has shown that changing threat contexts in the surveyed countries have in fact triggered shifts in the roles of their armed forces. Those threats include various climate change scenarios and their impact on already fragile regions and countries, especially in the form of potential increases in large-scale natural disasters; South-North, South-South and rural-urban migration due to instability, climate change and resulting changes to people's habitats and livelihoods; catastrophes resulting from a combination of natural and man-made disasters, such as the earthquake, tsunami and nuclear catastrophe in Japan; continuing threats from international terrorist networks; cyber insecurity; evolving terrorist threats; and political revolutions such as those currently experienced in the Middle East and North Africa.

These events have challenged and will continue to test societies' resolve. They will also test their ability to change "traditional" ways of responding to new and to a certain degree unpredictable threat scenarios by adjusting the instruments with which such threats are met. The armed forces, other security institutions and management and oversight institutions – and the societies whom they serve – will continue to face the challenge of finding a working balance that ensures both effective and legitimate responses to those threats. Learning from one's own and other countries' experiences – the ultimate aim of the mapping approach presented in this paper – might help in adjusting respective roles, functions and responsibilities. Finally, such an endeavour can help policy-makers and researchers maintain an accurate understanding of the current ways in which the armed forces are utilized and deployed, at home and in other countries. This is especially relevant as the armed forces continue to take on "non-traditional" roles that challenge common assumptions, perceptions and expectations.

NOTES

1   This SSR Paper emerges from a research project on "Mapping and Analysing Internal Roles of Armed Forces", carried out by the authors with the assistance of Ina Amann and Danail Hristov, and funded by the Directorate for Security and Defence Policy of the Swiss Federal Department of Defence, Civil Protection and Sports (DDPS). Initial conceptual work for this project was published as Albrecht Schnabel and Danail Hristov, "Conceptualising Non-traditional Roles and Tasks of Armed Forces", *S+F: Sicherheit und Frieden/Security and Peace*, vol. 28, no. 2, 2010, pp. 73–80. As indicated in the text, some passages of this paper draw on this first publication. The findings of the project were brought together in an internal report: Albrecht Schnabel, Ina Amann, Danail Hristov and Marc Krupanski, "Mapping and Analysing Internal Roles of Armed Forces: A Research Report, Report for the DDPS" (Geneva: DCAF, April 2011). We acknowledge and thank Ina Amann and Daniel Hristov for their research and written contributions to the project report, which served as the basis for this paper. We wish to acknowledge invaluable input provided by Pierre Aepli, Alan Bryden, Hans Born, Marc Caron, Robin Dyck, Timothy Edmunds, Cornelius Friesendorf, Guy de Haynin, Karl Haltiner, Heiner Hänggi, David Law, Michael Pope, Everett Summerfield, Arnold Teicht and Raphael Zaffran, as well as the participants at two consultation workshops on "Internal Roles of Armed Forces", 29 July 2010, and "Roles and Responsibilities of Security Institutions Revisited", 26 May 2011, both organized by the Geneva Centre for the Democratic Control of Armed Forces (DCAF). We thank Cherry Ekins for skilfully proofreading and copyediting the final text and Yury Korobovsky for handling the production of the publication. Finally, we are grateful to the series editors, Alan Bryden and Heiner Hänggi, for providing most helpful comments on earlier versions of this paper.

2   Timothy Edmunds, "What Are Armed Forces For? The Changing Nature of Military Roles in Europe", *International Affairs*, vol. 82, no. 6, 2006, p. 1059.

3   In the academic and policy literature as well as in policy and legal documents, the term "paramilitary forces" is often used to describe what are otherwise known as gendarmeries, carabinieries or home guards. Given the negative connotation attached to the term "paramilitaries" in many countries of the global South and the fact that those security troops are not always considered to be military forces, for the purpose of this project we use "gendarmeries" when referring to such intermediary forces – state security institutions that are, based on their mandates, roles and tasks, situated outside or between regular police services and armed forces.

4   Heiner Hänggi, "Making Sense of Security Sector Governance", in Heiner Hänggi and Theodor Winkler (eds), *Challenges of Security Sector Governance* (Münster: LIT, 2003). For a recent account of security sector reform and governance, as well as their implementation in real-world environments, see Hans Born and Albrecht Schnabel (eds), *Security Sector Reform in Challenging Environments* (Münster: LIT, 2009); Albrecht Schnabel and Hans Born, *Security Sector Reform: Narrowing the Gap between Theory and Practice*, SSR Paper No. 1 (Geneva: DCAF, 2011).

5   Timothy Edmunds, "What Are Armed Forces For?", p. 1062.

6   Ibid.

7   Ibid.

8   See, for instance, David Bayley, "The Police and Political Development in Europe", in Charles

Tilly (ed.), *The Formation of National States in Western Europe* (Princeton, NJ: Princeton University Press, 1975); Michael Broers, "Notabili, Gendarmes and the State: Preserving Order and the Origins of the Centralized State in the Italian Departments of the First Empire", in *Le pénal dans tous ses Etats* (Brussels: Facultés universitaires Saint-Louis, 1997), pp. 179–90; Charles Tilly, "War Making and State Making as Organized Crime", in Peter Evans, Dietrich Rueschemeyer and Theda Skocpol (eds), *Bringing the State Back In* (Cambridge: Cambridge University Press, 1985), pp. 169–91.

[9] See Keith Krause, *Towards a Practical Human Security Agenda*, DCAF Policy Paper No. 26 (Geneva: DCAF, 2007), p. 9.

[10] Charles Tilly, "War Making and State Making as Organized Crime".

[11] Keith Krause, *Towards a Practical Human Security Agenda*, p. 10.

[12] This and the following three paragraphs draw extensively on text in a previous publication of project findings. See Albrecht Schnabel and Danail Hristov, "Conceptualising Non-traditional Roles and Tasks of Armed Forces", pp. 74–5.

[13] See Barry Buzan, "Rethinking Security after the Cold War", *Cooperation and Conflict*, vol. 32, no. 1, 1997, p. 6.

[14] Timothy Edmunds, "What Are Armed Forces For?", p. 1062.

[15] Ibid. See also Samuel Huntington, "New Contingencies, Old Roles", *Joint Force Quarterly*, Spring 2003.

[16] Timothy Edmunds, "What Are Armed Forces For?", p. 1063.

[17] Ibid., p. 1064.

[18] Geoff Hoon, *Delivering Security in a Changing World: Defence White Paper* (London: Ministry of Defence, 2003), p. 3.

[19] Ibid., pp. 6–7.

[20] See also Hans Born and Aidan Wills, "The Roles of Armed Forces in Council of Europe Member States", European Commission for Democracy Through Law (Venice Commission), Study on Democratic Control of Armed Forces, Study No. 389, CDL-DEM(2007)009 (Strasbourg: Council of Europe, 26 September 2007).

[21] Albrecht Schnabel and Danail Hristov, "Conceptualising Non-traditional Roles and Tasks of Armed Forces", pp. 73–80.

[22] Royal Decree of 6 July 1994 on Operational Engagement of Military Forces and the Law of 20 May 1994, cited in Pierre d'Argent, "Military Law in Belgium", in Georg Nolte (ed.), *European Military Law Systems* (Berlin: De Gruyter Recht, 2003), pp. 191–3.

[23] See Ordinance No. 59-147 of January 1959; 1983 Decree No. 83-321 on the Prerogatives of Prefects in Terms of Non-Military Defence; Ministerial Instruction of 7 February establishing the SGDN; Ordinance 60-372 of 15 April 1960 on the State of Urgency; Inter-Ministerial Instruction No. 500/SGDN/MTS/OTP of 9 May 1995 on the Participation of the Military in Maintaining Public Order, cited in Jörg Gerkrath, "Military Law in France", in Georg Nolte (ed.), *European Military Law Systems* (Berlin: De Gruyter Recht, 2003), pp. 285–90.

[24] See Royal Decree 1125/1976, Organic Law 4/1981 on the Declaration of Emergency, Law 2/1985 of 21 January 1985 on Civil Protection, cited in Kim Eduard Lioe, *Armed Forces in Law Enforcement Operations? The German and European Perspectives* (Heidelberg: Springer, 2011), p. 108.

[25] See Emergency Powers Act 1920 and Emergency Powers Act 1964.

26   See Part XI of the National Defence Act (R.S. 1985, c. N-5), the Fisheries Act (R.S.C., 1985, c. F-14) and the Queen's Regulations and Orders.

27   See Statute of 11 July 1978, No. 382; Decree of 28 November 1997, No. 464, Art. 5(1); Law No. 331/2000 Article 1; Law of 24 February 1992, No. 225.

28   See Basic Law, Articles 87, 91, 35 paras 1 and 2, Article 87a, para. 2.

29   "The Oka Crisis", CBC Digital Archives, http://www.cbc.ca/archives/categories/politics/civil-unrest/the-oka-crisis-1/topic-the-oka-crisis.html

30   For instance, Jonathan Stevenson, "The Role of the Armed Forces of the United Kingdom in Securing the State against Terrorism", *Connections*, vol. 4, no. 3, 2005, pp. 121–33.

31   "Remembrance Day: Where They Fell", BBC, 10 November 2011, http://www.bbc.co.uk/news/uk-11743727; Malcolm Sutton, "Tabulations (Tables) of Basic Variables, An Index of Deaths from the Conflict in Ireland", University of Ulster, http://cain.ulst.ac.uk/sutton/tables/index.html

32   "Civil Contingencies", British Army, http://www.army.mod.uk/structure/13938.aspx

33   "Vigipirate et PPS", Ministère de la Défense, http://www.defense.gouv.fr/operations/france/vigipirate-pps; "Vigiliance, prévention, protection: le plan Vigipirate", Secrétariat Général de la Défense et de la Sécurité Nationale, http://www.sgdsn.gouv.fr/site_rubrique98.html

34   Carine Bobbera, "Le 200 000e militarie de Vigipirate honoré par le minister", Ministère de la Défense, 3 January 2012, http://www.defense.gouv.fr/actualites/articles/visite-du-ministre-a-vigipirate

35   "Germany to Allow Domestic Military Operations", *Daily Telegraph*, 17 August 2012, http://www.telegraph.co.uk/news/worldnews/europe/germany/9482870/Germany-to-allow-domestic-military-operations.html

36   "Vigipirate et PPS", Ministère de la Défense.

37   National Defence and the Canadian Forces, "Canada Command Backgrounder", BG #10.001, National Defence and the Canadian Forces, 12 January 2010.

38   Michael Head and Scott Mann, *Domestic Deployment of the Armed Forces: Military Powers, Law and Human Rights* (Surrey: Ashgate Publishing, 2009), p. 106.

39   Headquarters Department of Army, "Concept and Principles", in Field Manual 100-19, Domestic Support Operations, Department of Army, 1 July 1993.

40   Michael Head and Scott Mann, *Domestic Deployment of the Armed Forces*, p. 106.

41   Elisabetta Povoledo, "Italy Begins Military Effort to Quell Crime", *New York Times*, 5 August 2008, http://www.nytimes.com/2008/08/05/world/europe/05italy.html?_r=0

42   Johann Frank, "A Neutral's Perspective: The Role of the Austrian Armed Forces in Homeland Security", *Connections*, vol. 4, no. 3, 2005, p. 99.

43   Austria Defence and Sport Ministry, *Weissbuch 2008* (Vienna: Amtliche Publikation der Republik Österreich/Bundesminister für Landesverteidigung und Sport, 2009), p. 37, http://www.bmlv.gv.at/pdf_pool/publikationen/weissbuch_2008.pdf

44   Pieter De Crem, *Politieke Oriëntatienota*, Belgian Ministry of Defence, 2008, p. 12, http://www.mil.be/modnew/doc/viewdoc.asp?LAN=nl&FILE=&ID=1803

45   Federal Constitution Act, Article 79 B-VG, Sec. 2 WG 2001.

46   Danish Defence Act on the Purpose, Task and Organisation of the Armed Forces, Law No. 122 of 27 February 2001 and in force since 1 March 2001.

47 "NorthCOM Helping Out", KKTV.com, 18 October 2002, http://www.kktv.com/news/headlines/126106.html; Scott Elliott, "Eberhart Briefs Congress on U.S. Northern Command", US Northern Command, 14 March 2003, http://www.northcom.mil/News/2003/031403.html

48 Andrew Crosby, "Military, Mounties Trained for the Games", *The Dominion*, 18 February 2010, http://www.dominionpaper.ca/articles/2946

49 "04/06/10 – Protection militaire du XXVe sommet Afrique France", Ministère de la Défense, last modified 9 July 2010, http://www.defense.gouv.fr/operations/missions-interieures/autres-missint/04-06-10-protection-militaire-du-xxve-sommet-afrique-france

50 Andrew Crosby, "Military, Mounties Trained for the Games".

51 "Building and Personal Security", *Washington Post*, http://projects.washingtonpost.com/top-secret-america/functions/security/

52 "Commandement Militaire de la Région Bruxelles Capitale", Défense Belge, http://www.mil.be/ops-trg/units/index.asp?LAN=fr&ID=790

53 Michael Head and Scott Mann, *Domestic Deployment of the Armed Forces*, p. 106.

54 "1980: SAS Rescue Ends Iran Embassy Siege", BBC *Home On This Day*, http://news.bbc.co.uk/ onthisday/hi/dates/stories/may/5/newsid_2510000/2510873.stm

55 See, for instance, Benjamin S. Buckland, Fred Schreier and Theodor H. Winkler, *Democratic Governance Challenges of Cyber Security*, DCAF Horizon 2015 Working Paper No. 1 (Geneva: DCAF, 2009); Fred Schreier, Barbara Weekes and Theodor H. Winkler, *Cyber Security: The Road Ahead*, DCAF Horizon 2015 Working Paper No. 4 (Geneva: DCAF, 2011); Fred Schreier, *On Cyberwarfare*, DCAF Horizon 2015 Working Paper No. 7 (Geneva: DCAF, 2012).

56 Thom Shanker, "Pentagon Will Help Homeland Security Department Fight Domestic Cyberattacks", *New York Times*, 20 October 2010, http://www.nytimes.com/2010/ 10/21/us/21cyber.html

57 "Vigipirate et PPS", Ministère de la Défense.

58 Richard Warnes, "France", in Brian A. Jackson (ed.), *Considering the Creation of a Domestic Intelligence Agency in the United States: Lessons from the Experiences of Australia, Canada, France, Germany, and the United Kingdom* (Santa Monica, CA: RAND, 2009).

59 Eric Lichtblau and Mark Mazzetti, "Military Expands Intelligence Role in U.S.", *New York Times*, 14 January 2007, http://www.nytimes.com/2007/01/14/washington/14spy.html?pagewanted=print

60 Norwegian Ministry of Defence, "Capable Force: Strategic Concept for the Norwegian Armed Forces", 2009, p. 59, http://www.regjeringen.no/upload/FD/Dokumenter/Capable-force_strategic-concept.pdf

61 "Disaster Preparedness", *Washington Post*, http://projects.washingtonpost.com/top-secret-america/functions/disaster-preparation/

62 See, for example, Spencer S. Hsu, "Agencies Clash on Military's Border Role", *Washington Post*, 28 June 2009, http://www.washingtonpost.com/wp-dyn/content/article/2009/06/27/AR2009062700956.html; Patrick Martin, "Pentagon to Deploy 20,000 Troops on Domestic 'Anti-Terror' Mission", *Wall Street Journal*, 2 December 2008.

63 "Contaminated Water Crisis Continues in Nokia", *Helsingin Sanomat*, http://www.hs.fi/english/article/Contaminated+water+crisis+continues+in+Nokia/1135232419868

64   Angelique Chrisafis, "How the Brigadier Has Mopped Up Chaos and Won Farmers' Support", *The Guardian*, 29 March 2001, http://www.guardian.co.uk/uk/2001/mar/30/ footandmouth. angeliquechrisafis

65   Civil Contingencies Secretariat, "Backgrounder on Civil Contingencies Act 2004", Cabinet Office, http://www.cabinetoffice.gov.uk/media/132428/15mayshortguide.pdf

66   "Luxembourg, General Information", NATO Allied Command Operations, http://www.aco.nato.int/page127301514.aspx

67   "Red River Rising: Manitoba Floods – A State of Emergency", CBC Digital Archives, http://www.cbc.ca/archives/categories/environment/extreme-weather/red-river-rising-manitoba- floods/topic---red-river-rising-manitoba-floods.html

68   See, for example, "El desastre ecológico de Aznalcóllar", Universidad de Granada Departamento de Edafología y Química Agrícola, 1 September 2010, http://edafologia.ugr.es/donana/aznal.htm

69   Austria's constitution can be found in full at http://www.wienerzeitung.at/linkmap/recht/ verfassung1.htm

70   Johann Frank, "A Neutral's Perspective", p. 99.

71   J. Luther, "Military Law in Italy", in Georg Nolte (ed.), *European Military Law Systems* (Berlin: De Gruyter Recht, 2003), p. 437.

72   "Environmental Work", Swedish Armed Forces, http://www.forsvarsmakten.se/en/About-the-Armed-Forces/Enviroment/

73   Ibid.

74   "Danish Defence, Aims and Tasks", Defence Command Denmark, http://forsvaret.dk/FKO/ eng/Facts%20and%20Figures/Aim%20and%20tasks/Pages/default.aspx

75   "The SAR Mission", United States Coast Guard, http://www.uscg.mil/hq/cg5/cg534/

76   "30/06/08: Les armées évacuent d'urgence un enfant de Corse vers le continent", Ministère de la Défense, last modified 7 July 2010, http://www.defense.gouv.fr/operations/missions-interieures/autres-missint/30-06-08-les-armees-evacuent-d-urgence-un-enfant-de-corse-vers-le-continent

77   "French Military Steps Up Search for Bodies, Black Boxes of Crashed Plane", *China View*, 11 June 2009, http://news.xinhuanet.com/english/2009-06/11/content_11525994.htm

78   See, for instance, White Paper Commission, *The French White Paper on Defence and National Security* (Paris: Odile Jacob, 2008), http://merln.ndu.edu/whitepapers/ France_English2008.pdf; Jörg Gerkrath, "Military Law in France", in Georg Nolte (ed.), *European Military Law Systems* (Berlin: De Gruyter Recht, 2003), pp. 275–336.

79   "Royal Netherlands Air Force, Tasks", Ministry of Defence, http://www.defensie.nl/english/ air_force/tasks/

80   "Building and Personal Security", *Washington Post*, http://projects.washingtonpost.com/ top-secret-america/; "Training", *Washington Post*, http://projects.washingtonpost.com/top-secret-america/functions/training/

81   "Military Exercises to Be Conducted in the Downtown Area", Los Angeles Police Department press release, 23 January 2012, http://www.lapdonline.org/newsroom/news_view/50045

82   The Act is available online at http://www.finlex.fi/en/laki/kaannokset/2007/en20070551.pdf

83   Norwegian Ministry of Defence, "Capable Force", p. 59.

84   J. Luther, "Military Law in Italy", p. 437.

85   Scott Elliott, "Eberhart Briefs Congress on U.S. Northern Command".

86 "Danish Defence, Aim and Tasks", Defence Command Denmark.

87 The law is available online, in Finnish, http://www.finlex.fi/fi/laki/ajantasa/1995/19951251

88 Public Information Division of Defence Command, *The Finnish Defence Forces Annual Report 2008* (Helsinki: Finnish Defence Command, 2009), p. 16, http://www.puolustusvoimat.fi/wcm/c1072b0042c0efdbaae1ba55d4d4b8c9/toimintakertomus_2008_eng.pdf?MOD=AJPER ES

89 Laurence M. Hickey, "Enhancing the Naval Mandate for Law Enforcement: Hot Pursuit or Hot Potato?", National Defence and the Canadian Forces, modified 14 July 2008, http://www.journal.forces.gc.ca/vo7/no1/maritime-marin-eng.asp

90 See, for instance, Ministry of Defence, "A Usable and Accessible Defence Force – The Policy's Orientation" (Stockholm: Government Offices of Sweden, 2010), http://www.sweden.gov.se/content/1/c6/13/77/05/1705333d.pdf

91 "Royal Netherlands Navy, Tasks", Ministry of Defence, http://www.defensie.nl/english/navy/tasks

92 "The Danish Ice Service in General", Admiral Danish Fleet, http://www.forsvaret.dk/SOK/eng/ National/Ice/Pages/default.aspx

93 J. Luther, "Military Law in Italy", p. 437.

94 Ibid.

95 "About Us", US Army Corps of Engineers, http://www.usace.army.mil/About.aspx

96 Deployment outside the subsidiary threshold, including for harvest support, is articulated within Artikel 87a, Abs.2 GG: Amtshilfe, available online at http://www.iuscomp.org/gla/statutes/GG.htm

97 "Jeunesse à la Défense", Défense Belge, http://www.mil.be/ipr/subject/index.asp? LAN=fr &ID=217

98 Swedish Armed Forces, *The Pocket Guide to the Swedish Armed Forces 2009* (Stockholm: Swedish Armed Forces Public Relations Office, 2009), p. 34.

99 "Danish Defence, Aims and Tasks", Defence Command Denmark.

100 "Royal Netherlands Army, National Tasks", Ministry of Defence, http://www.defensie.nl/english/army/tasks/national_tasks/; "Royal Netherlands Army, Tasks", Ministry of Defence, http://www.defensie.nl/english/army/tasks/

101 "Les missions de l'Armée", Lëtzebuerger Arméi, http://www.armee.lu/organisation/missions _armee/

102 For further discussions on the utility and motivations to engage in non-traditional roles, see Juan G. Ayala, *What Else Should Our Military Forces Be Doing? The Benefits of Participating in Military Operations Other than War* (Newport, RI: Naval War College, 2000), http://handle.dtic.mil/100.2/ADA381713; Nogues Thierry Chevrier and Stéhane Sauvage André, "Armées et sécurité intérieure: Perception des acteurs institutionnels civils et militaire", LARES-Université Rennes 2-C2SD, May 2001, http://www.c2sd.sga.defense.gouv.fr/IMG/pdf/armee_securite_int_10_01.pdf; Nogues Thierry, "Armées et missions de sécurité intérieure", *Doctrine*, no. 6, March 2005, http://www.cdef.terre. defense.gouv.fr/publications/doctrine/doctrine06/version_fr/libre_reflex/art_17.pdf

103 "Military Expenditure (% of GDP)", World Bank, http://data.worldbank.org/indicator/MS.MIL.XPND.GD.ZS

104 See, for example, Anthony Forster, *Armed Forces and Society in Europe* (Basingstoke: Palgrave Macmillan, 2005), p. 167.

[105] "Top Secret America", *Washington Post*, http://projects.washingtonpost.com/top-secret-america/articles/

[106] Quoted in Jonathan Stevenson, "The Role of the Armed Forces of the United Kingdom in Securing the State against Terrorism", p. 129.

[107] *Operations in the UK: The Defence Contribution to Resilience*, Joint Doctrine Publication 02, 2nd edn (Swindon: Development, Concepts and Doctrine Centre, Ministry of Defence, September 2007), p. v, para. 2.

[108] Michael Head and Scott Mann, *Domestic Deployment of the Armed Forces*, p. 95.

[109] Heike Krieger and Georg Nolte, "Military Law in Germany", in Georg Nolte (ed.), *European Military Law Systems* (Berlin: De Gruyter Recht, 2003), p. 353.

[110] The Norwegian constitution is available online at http://www.stortinget.no/en/In-English/About-the-Storting/The-Constitution/The-Constitution/

[111] Lorenzo Cotino Hueso, "Military Law in Spain", in Georg Nolte (ed.), *European Military Law Systems* (Berlin: De Gruyter Recht, 2003), p. 714.

[112] The reconstruction era in the US lasted from 1865 to 1877 following the US Civil War. In short, the era involved a series of policies and efforts launched by the federal government to re-establish self-government of southern states and their incorporation into the federal system of governance, as well as attempts to secure the civil rights of formerly enslaved African-Americans. The federal government deployed the armed forces to occupy southern states in order to enforce the reconstruction policies. The Compromise of 1877 marked an end to reconstruction through a deal that settled the disputed 1876 presidential election by granting the Republican candidate presidency under the condition that the occupation of southern states would end and all armed forces would be removed.

[113] See Law 42/1999 regulating the statute of the Guardia Civil; Organic Law 2/1986 on Security Forces; Organic Law 11/1991 on the Disciplinary Regime of the Guardia Civil.

[114] See Law 2009-971 of 3 August 2009 relative to the Gendarmerie Nationale.

[115] Brent C. Bankus, "Volunteer Military Forces Provide Homeland Security Around the World", *State Defence Monograph Series*, Special Units Issue, Fall 2007, p. 10, http://www.dtic.mil/cgi-bin/GetTRDoc?Location=U2&doc=GetTRDoc.pdf&AD=ADA504904

[116] Ibid.

[117] See, for instance, J. Luther, "Military Law in Italy", p. 437; "22/05/08: Les militaries retrouvent une jeune fille dans l'Aude", Ministère de la Défense, http://www.defense.gouv.fr/operations/missions-interieures/autres-missint/22-05-08-les-militaires-retrouvent-une-jeune-fille-dans-l-aude; "Feux de forêts", Ministère de la Défense, modified 8 July 2010, http://www.defense.gouv.fr/operations/missions-interieures/feux-de-forets; "Actualités", Ministère de la Défense, modified 8 July 2010, http://www.defense. gouv.fr/operations/missions-interieures/intemperies/actualites

[118] The Canada First Defence Strategy is the national military recruitment, professionalization and mission strategy doctrine developed by Prime Minister Stephen Harper in 2008. More information can be found at http://www.forces.gc.ca/site/pri/first-premier/index-eng.asp

[119] Andrew Crosby, "Military, Mounties Trained for the Games".

[120] "Emergency Management Response", Public Safety Canada, http://www.publicsafety.gc.ca/prg/em/res-eng.aspx

[121] See Act on the Defence Forces 11.5.2007/551, section 2, available at http://www.finlex.fi/en/laki/kaannokset/2007/en20070551.pdf

122 These are available at http://www.deutsches–wehrrecht.de/Einsatz_Streitkräfte.pdf
123 "Flooding in Lower Austria", Ministry of Defence and Sports, 20 April 2006, http://www.bmlv. gv.at/english/dynmod/artikel.php?id=1801
124 "Tasks of the Danish Emergency Management Agency", Danish Ministry of Defence, http://www.fmn.dk/eng/allabout/Pages/ResponsibilitiesoftheEmergencyManagement Agency.aspx
125 National Defence and the Canadian Forces, "Canada Command Backgrounder".
126 See Keith Krause, *Towards a Practical Human Security Agenda*, pp. 11–15; Anthony Forster, *Armed Forces and Society in Europe*, p. 160.
127 According to Huntington, for instance, additional tasks for the military should not impair the army's main mission, which is warfare. See Samuel Huntington, "New Contingencies, Old Roles".
128 See Albrecht Schnabel and Hans Born, *Security Sector Reform*.